PROGRAM STYLE, DESIGN, EFFICIENCY, DEBUGGING, AND TESTING

PROGRAM STYLE, DESIGN, EFFICIENCY, DEBUGGING, AND TESTING

DENNIE VAN TASSEL

University of California
Santa Cruz, California

PRENTICE-HALL, INC.

Englewood Cliffs, N.J.

Library of Congress Cataloging in Publication Data

Van Tassel, Dennie,
    Program style, design, efficiency, debugging and
testing.

    Includes bibliographies.
    1. Electronic digital computers--Programming.
2. Debugging in computer science. 3. Computer
programs--Testing. I. Title.
QA76.6.V37   001.6'42   74-3377
ISBN 0-13-729939-7

© 1974 by
PRENTICE-HALL, INC.
Englewood Cliffs, N.J.

10 9 8 7 6 5 4 3

Printed in the United States of America

PRENTICE-HALL INTERNATIONAL, INC., *London*
PRENTICE-HALL OF AUSTRALIA, PTY., LTD., *Sydney*
PRENTICE-HALL OF CANADA, LTD., *Toronto*
PRENTICE-HALL OF INDIA PRIVATE LIMITED, *New Delhi*
PRENTICE-HALL OF JAPAN, INC., *Tokyo*

For my wife,
Cynthia

Contents

Preface

This book is written for those who already know how to program but wish to increase their programming proficiency. The contents cover five subjects that are seldom discussed in beginning programming books: the style or readability of programs, program design, efficiency or optimization of programs, debugging, and testing. These subjects are usually left for the programmer to learn by experience. While experience is a good teacher, it is also rather slow and hap-haphazard, leaving much to chance. Most programmers have enough to learn by experience without leaving these important programming subjects for that slow process, too. In addition to the five topics mentioned, a very large number of programming problems are included.

Most of the information collected in this book could be classified as the "Lore of Programming." This information is known to some very experienced programmers in bits and pieces, but has not been collected together as an organized body of knowledge. In his ACM Turing Lecture several years ago, Dr. R. W. Hamming suggested that a style manual for programmers was needed.

This is my attempt to compile such a manual. I hope that I have made a fairly complete survey of the "Lore of Programming," but I am sure I have overlooked some things. Thus, I would be happy to hear from my readers any suggestions they might like to contribute to the "Lore of Programming."

Special thanks to Frank DeRemer from whom I have learned a great deal about programming style. Also, special thanks to Bill McKeeman who let me use some of his problems and who also taught me a great deal. Lastly, thanks to Harry Huskey who has employed me and put up with me while I wrote this book.

DENNIE VAN TASSEL

PROGRAM STYLE, DESIGN, EFFICIENCY, DEBUGGING, AND TESTING

The purpose of programming is not the program,
but the result of the computation.

Alas there are no prizes for coding;
the results are what count.

I

Program Style

The day may come when computers write programs for other computers, or we may someday be able to write programs in English. But until this happens, we will have to concern ourselves with the dynamics of producing programs which other people can read. Not many people will argue with the simple request that a programmer should at least be able to read his own program. This is where programming style enters the scene.

Programming style is concerned with the readability of programs. If each programmer uses his own "style" of programming, his programs may be incomprehensible to others. Thus, style has to do with a selection of programming habits or techniques that appeal to experienced programmers because the habits produce programs that are correct, efficient, maintainable, and readable. The rules of good style are the result of consensus among experienced programmers. Once a programmer becomes accustomed to a certain style, his own programs and other people's programs will be more easily understood. If every programmer used his own particular style, a garbled tower of Babel would result.

The main purpose of a program is to be read by humans rather than machines. People must read and understand the program in order to correct, maintain, and modify it. If we were concerned only with the machine, programs would be written so machines could read them easier than people could. Programs are also documents for future reference, they are educational media for instruction on coded algorithms, and they are used for further development of better programs. Thus we insist that program languages be conducive to producing readable statements. Too often the desirability of readability is forgotten in the haste to get the program working.

It is doubtful if anyone would argue that it is not important whether a program is readable or not. The original programmer must always be able to read his own program. Thus, guidelines of programming style will also help him. Conventional language uses punctuation, paragraphing, ordering, and spacing to improve readability. Programming languages can use similar aids to avoid abstruse programs.

Abstruse programs are usually very difficult to modify. This is especially true if the original programmer does not do the modification. An unfortunate result is that it is usually easier to rewrite a program than modify someone else's program. Program specifications are usually in a constant state of flux. Often we not only don't know what we want, but after getting results we want the program changed. The tendency is to begin a program with modest ambitions and expand it continuously. If program style guidelines are followed, some of the abstruseness in programs will disappear.

When a programmer can pick up someone else's program and see that it is organized and easy to read, the normal reluctance and confusion of updating or modification starts to disappear. A readable program creates the impression that the original coder knew what he was doing.

If the programs are coded for an organization, the adoption of an agreed-on style will help make the programs the property of the organization instead of the private property of a single programmer.

STANDARDS OF STYLE

An argument against standards of programming style is the following: "Programming style is a matter of personal opinion and preference, and thus should not be restricted." This argument simply says that chaos is better than order.

The rule for standards is:

If there is more than one way to do something and the choice is rather arbitrary, pick one way and always do it that way.

The advantages of this philosophy are:

By eliminating arbitrary parameters, communication can be more precise. By doing the same thing in the same way each time, communication is less susceptible to misunderstanding.

The disadvantages of standards are:

1. They might restrict future growth and progress.
2. They might be too restrictive for universal usage.
3. They might be too cumbersome for universal use.

In the last two cases the standards are just ignored. The standards of style given here are simply a product of common sense and common usage by experienced programmers and are not meant to be restrictive.

COMMENTS

It seems that the desirability of comments should be self-evident, but they aren't always included in programs. Comments are left out to save time or keypunching, or "they will be put in later." These excuses are not very good because in a surprisingly short time even the original programmer will find he has forgotten many of the details of the program. A program with explanatory comments is much easier to debug. When looking at someone else's program, a colleague often is forced to spend many hours tracing the program logic or simply rewriting the undocumented program when a change is necessary. In such a case all the original time "saved" is used up many times over.

It is generally a good rule to write comments in as you write the program. Then you are most familiar with the details. Later on it will be difficult to remember what should be commented. A general rule is: the more comments the better. Very few programs are over commented.

There are two types of comments: Prologue comments and explanatory comments.

Prologue Comments

It is useful for each program, subroutine, paragraph, or procedure to have some statements at the beginning to explain what it does. The minimum expectations are:

1. A description of what the program does.
2. Usage: How to call it or use it.
3. A list and explanation of the important variables or arrays.
4. Instructions on input/output. List any files.
5. A list of subroutines used.
6. The name of any special scientific methods used along with a reference where more information can be found.
7. Some indication of how long it takes.
8. Amount of core needed.
9. Special operating requirements.
10. Author.
11. Date Written.

All this information must be supplied for documentation, and the best place to put it is right in the program so it can be easily found. The program should be its own documentation. Figure 1.1 shows sample prologue documentation.

Explanatory Comments

Explanatory comments are inserted in the program to explain any code that is not obvious by just reading the code. Comments should be put before important loops or branches, indicating what is being done. Properly done comments provide a narrative account of the flow of data and logic in the program. Provide comments whenever you do something which may not be entirely obvious to another person. This documentation will then be carried along as part of the

```
C                                                                         TALL   10
C*************************************************************************TALL   20
C                                                                         TALL   30
C         SUBROUTINE TALLY                                                TALL   40
C                                                                         TALL   50
C         PURPOSE                                                         TALL   60
C            CALCULATE TOTAL, MEAN, STANDARD DEVIATION, MINIMUM, MAXIMUM  TALL   70
C            FOR EACH VARIABLE IN A SET (OR A SUBSET) OF OBSERVATIONS.    TALL   80
C                                                                         TALL   90
C         USAGE                                                           TALL  100
C            CALL TALLY(A,S,TOTAL,AVER,SD,VMIN,VMAX,NO,NV,IER)            TALL  110
C                                                                         TALL  120
C         DESCRIPTION OF PARAMETERS                                       TALL  130
C            A      - OBSERVATION MATRIX, NO BY NV.                       TALL  140
C            S      - INPUT VECTOR INDICATING SUBSET OF A. ONLY THOSE     TALL  150
C                     OBSERVATIONS WITH A NON-ZERO S(J) ARE CONSIDERED.   TALL  160
C                     VECTOR LENGTH IS NO.                                TALL  170
C            TOTAL  - OUTPUT VECTOR OF TOTALS OF EACH VARIABLE. VECTOR    TALL  180
C                     LENGTH IS NV.                                       TALL  190
C            AVER   - OUTPUT VECTOR OF AVERAGES OF EACH VARIABLE. VECTOR  TALL  200
C                     LENGTH IS NV.                                       TALL  210
C            SD     - OUTPUT VECTOR OF STANDARD DEVIATIONS OF EACH        TALL  220
C                     VARIABLE. VECTOR LENGTH IS NV.                      TALL  230
C            VMIN   - OUTPUT VECTOR OF MINIMA OF EACH VARIABLE. VECTOR    TALL  240
C                     LENGTH IS NV.                                       TALL  250
C            VMAX   - OUTPUT VECTOR OF MAXIMA OF EACH VARIABLE. VECTOR    TALL  260
C                     LENGTH IS NV.                                       TALL  270
C            NO     - NUMBER OF OBSERVATIONS.                             TALL  280
C            NV     - NUMBER OF VARIABLES FOR EACH OBSERVATION.           TALL  290
C            IER    - ZERO, IF NO ERROR.                                  TALL  300
C                   - 1, IF S IS NULL.  VMIN=-1.E75, VMAX=SD=AVER=1.E75.  TALL  310
C                   - 2, IF S HAS ONLY ONE NON-ZERO ELEMENT. VMIN=VMAX.   TALL  320
C                     SD=0.0                                              TALL  330
C                                                                         TALL  340
C         REMARKS                                                         TALL  350
C            NONE                                                         TALL  360
C                                                                         TALL  370
C         SUBROUTINES AND FUNCTION SUBPROGRAMS REQUIRED                   TALL  380
C            NONE                                                         TALL  390
C                                                                         TALL  400
C         METHOD                                                          TALL  410
C            ALL OBSERVATIONS CORRESPONDING TO A NON-ZERO ELEMENT IN S    TALL  420
C            VECTOR ARE ANALYZED FOR EACH VARIABLE IN MATRIX A.           TALL  430
C            TOTALS ARE ACCUMULATED AND MINIMUM AND MAXIMUM VALUES ARE    TALL  440
C            FOUND. FOLLOWING THIS, MEANS AND STANDARD DEVIATIONS ARE     TALL  450
C            CALCULATED.  THE DIVISOR FOR STANDARD DEVIATION IS ONE LESS  TALL  460
C            THAN THE NUMBER OF OBSERVATIONS USED.                        TALL  470
C                                                                         TALL  480
C                                                                         TALL  490
C         REFERENCE                                                       TALL  500
C            STATISTICS  BY MURRAY R. SPIEGEL                             TALL  510
C            SCHAUM PUBLISHING COMPANY                                    TALL  520
C                                                                         TALL  530
C         TIME-REQUIRED                                                   TALL  540
C            FOR 10 VARIABLES 20 SECONDS.                                 TALL  550
C            FOR 20 VARIABLES 45 SECONDS.                                 TALL  560
C            FOR 65 VARIABLES 95 SECONDS.                                 TALL  570
C                                                                         TALL  580
C                                                                         TALL  590
C         SIZE                                                            TALL  600
C            199 CARDS.                                                   TALL  610



C            OBJECT CODE  1960.                                           TALL  620
C                                                                         TALL  630
C                                                                         TALL  640
C         PROGRAMMER                                                      TALL  650
C            ABE SURECODER.                                               TALL  660
C                                                                         TALL  670
C         DATE-WRITTEN                                                    TALL  680
C            JULY 1972.                                                   TALL  690
C                                                                         TALL  700
C*************************************************************************TALL  710
C                                                                         TALL  720
```

Figure 1.1

5

program itself. It can help a new programmer understand your program or help you understand earlier sections of the program while new parts are being written. A good rule might be a minimum of one comment every 10 lines of code for high-level languages.

High-level languages are designed to be as readable and self-documenting as possible, but quite often the logic used by the programmer is not apparent to someone else reading the program. In such cases (and such cases are far more prevalent than programmers realize) comments are invaluable. If you were to read the program to a new programmer, you should have a comment in each place where you would have to stop to explain the coding to the new programmer.

The type of comment used is important. You should assume the reader is familiar with the language of the program. Therefore, comments should explain the purpose of a group of program statements, not describe the operation of the statements. For example:

```
/* BRANCH IF LESS THAN ZERO */
```

The above it not a good comment since the person reading the program would know the programming language and be able to ascertain that a negative branch was to take place. But he wouldn't know why —which is what comments are supposed to tell him. Instead, this type of comment should be used:

```
/*BRANCH TO NEGATIVE ACCOUNT PROCESSING IF TOTAL COSTS
       ARE LESS THAN ZERO.        */
```

The above comment tells why a negative branch is to be used. Comments should not explain programming language syntax, but should indicate the purpose or what is happening in the logic of the program.

A test of commenting is that a programmer should be able to read only the comments and understand what the program is doing without referring to any other documentation. Another test can be made for adequate comments by using an automatic flowcharter. An automatic flowcharter is a program that reads a source program and prints a flowchart from the source program. A high-quality flowchart of proper detail can be produced only from a listing that has been properly commented. Thus, a program flowcharter allows an automatic test of sufficient comments.

Placement of Comments

When using an assembly language, add a comment on each line. Comments that are interspersed in the coding are easier to read when they are preceded and followed by a blank line. An additional method to set off comments is to make a box of special characters. Then this box can be used in several ways:

(a) To create a box in which the comments appear.
(b) To group a set of commands. This is done by placing a comment line filled with special characters before and after the group of comments.
(c) To set up a boundary which indicates one comment applies to several lines of code.

In Fig. 1.1 a comment line of asterisks is used above and below the comments to form a box for the comments.

BLANK LINES

Blank space is an often overlooked method of improving the appearance of a program. Blank lines can be used for vertical spacing. Blank lines are used in English to separate paragraphs. Likewise you can use blank lines to separate elements of your program. A single blank line can be used to separate each similar group of statements, and several blank lines should be used to separate any major section of the program. The use of blank lines will make any search for the major routines within a program much easier.

A blank line should follow any unconditional transfer of control to indicate a break in program flow. Blank lines before and after comments make the comments stand out more. Blank lines can be created by blank cards in a source deck or blank comment lines.

COBOL, PL/I, FORTRAN, and assembly language have special commands which control carriage spacing on source statements. COBOL users can use EJECT, SKIP1, SKIP2, and SKIP3. PL/I users can specify a control column using job control language which will control spacing in the source listing. The WATFIV

version of FORTRAN has the $EJECT and $SPACE available for
vertical spacing.

The skipping to a new page is similar to beginning a new chapter
in a book. Both indicate a larger change than just a blank line
(new paragraph). Blank space separates the program into mean-
ingful units.

BLANK SPACES

In programming languages blank spaces are quite often optional.
But it makes no more sense to leave out all blank space in pro-
grams than it would to leave out blank spaces in written text.
Icouldalwayswritelikethisandyoucanreaditbutittakestoomucheffort.
Blanks should be left in all places that will improve the readability
of the program.

It is possible to write statements like this:

```
DO10I=1,23,2
```

But the following is much easier to read

```
DO 10 I = 1, 23, 2
```

Liberal usage of blanks will add significantly to the readability of
programs. Include blank spaces between items in data lists, and before and after arithmetic operators (+, -, =). Sometimes blanks
are desirable before and after the two operations (*, /).

IDENTIFICATION AND SEQUENCE NUMBERING

Most programming languages allow for the identification and sequence numbering of the source program in columns 73-80. Identification is normally punched in columns 73-76 and then columns
77-80 can be used for sequence numbering. Sequence numbering
should be in increments of 10 in order to allow the inserting of new
cards. COBOL programs should be sequenced in columns 1-6, then
columns 73-80 can be used for identification.

Sequence numbering helps prevent errors due to programs being out of order. A careless operator could easily drop a program deck and "attempt" to put the deck back in order. Thus, the programmer will usually have no indication that his program deck has been shuffled if it is not numbered sequentially.

Sequenced source programs are helpful when debugging because the sequence number can be used to locate a card in a large deck quickly. Thus, the programmer should sequence the number source programs when first coding them. Sequence numbering and identification make a program look neater and more complete and thus psychologically appear more readable.

In order to encourage sequential numbering of source programs every computer installation should provide a program to reproduce and sequence source decks. Then an interpreting keypunch can be used to interpret the new source deck. Figure 1.1 shows a program that has identification and sequence numbering.

SELECTION OF VARIABLE NAMES

Variable names should be selected to best identify the symbolic quantities they represent. If there are no restrictions on name size, use names as long as necessary and not longer than necessary. For example:

$$X = Y + Z$$

has little mnemonic value and the variable names are poorly selected. The following is much better:

$$PRICE = COST + PROFIT$$

Proper selection of variable names is the most important principle in program readability. It is also the easiest and least expensive technique since it usually takes just a little thought by the programmer and costs no more in machine time.

Selection of suggestive names should also be used when naming programs, paragraphs, procedures, functions, and subroutines. If the program labels match labels you used in flowcharts or analysis, then you can relate them to these earlier procedural forms. Variable names should be selected that are prevalent in the subject area of the application.

It is easy to pick good variable names in COBOL and PL/I since both allow long names and have a separator character. FORTRAN is severely limited by short lengths for variable names (anywhere from 5-8 characters in different versions) and its absence of a separator character. ALGOL allows long variable names but has no separator character, so all words must be run together. "Cute" names that have no bearing on the task involved become completely unintelligible later when the program has grown "cold" or when a new programmer must modify the program.

Here is one way you can pick a good symbolic variable name: When choosing variable names try stating what the variable is to stand for in an English sentence and then pick the most important word.

Some programming languages have no reserved words. This permits the programmer to use any word as a variable name, even those normally used as commands. For example:

FORTRAN

```
      DO 5 I6 = 1.34
14 FORMAT(I6) = I
 5 END = K*I
```

PL/I

```
IF IF = THEN THEN THEN = ELSE;
       ELSE ELSE = IF;
```

All of these are legal statements and unambiguous to the compiler, but notice how difficult they are to interpret because of predetermined meanings for the variable names. Thus you should avoid using words that could confuse the reader.

Different types (that is, integer, real, complex, character) are often a menace to the programmer. However, this is no staggering disadvantage since such faults are usually easy to find, especially if the programmer adopts some naming convention in his mnemonics to identify types that are conceptually different to him. For example, in a program that uses a few complex variables, all complex variable names could start with C or CMP. This prefix would remind you that the variable is a complex variable. A similar technique can be used to help identify files.

    Programs can be nicely written

```
IF CONTENTS(PITCHER) < QUART THEN
    FILL(PITCHER)
ELSE
    POUR(PITCHER)
```

or they can be poorly written:

```
    IF      XCONT (PTCH
)    <       QT    THEN  XFILL    (
     PTCH
)   ELSE                XPOUR    (
        PTCH)
```

FILE NAMES

    When working with files in languages such as COBOL and PL/I it is a good idea to select a prefix to identify each file. Then you can use this prefix on every subordinate item in the file description. In this example, MASTER is used as the prefix.

COBOL

```
FILE SECTION.
FD  MASTER-FILE,
    .
    .
    .
01  MASTER-RECORD.
    03 MASTER-NAME      PICTURE X(20).
    03 MASTER-ADDRESS   PICTURE X(40).
    03 MASTER-NUMBER    PICTURE 9(08).
    .
    .
    .
WORKING-STORAGE SECTION.
01  MASTER-WORK-AREA.
    05 MASTER-COUNT     PICTURE 9(04).
```

If each file has a unique prefix, it is much easier to read the program. The prefix will help locate the field in the program listing and indicate which fields and work areas are together logically.

This technique allows for prefixes on identical names, such as a date field. For example:

```
MASTER-DATE
TRANSACTION-DATE
REPORT-DATE
```

Even though three different date fields are used, each one is easy to identify because of the prefix. If you do not use the prefix method you are forced to use different abbreviations such as DATE, DTE, DAT which do not adequately label the fields.

When selecting record names use record-oriented names, instead of job-oriented names. The following names are job-oriented:

```
01   OUTPUT-FILE
     05 OUTPUT-NAME
     05 OUTPUT-ADDRESS
```

These names would be usable only once, that is, when the file is an output file. On the next job the record might be an input file and the above labels would not make sense.

By more careful selection of names the same record names can be used in several interconnected programs. For example:

```
01   MASTER-FILE
     05 MASTER-NAME
     05 MASTER-ADDRESS
```

The above record name can be used for the record in every program which might use the record.

The use of the same names for identical files in different programs means programmers can immediately identify the file. Program managers might find it advantageous to set up a standard file label when one file is used in many programs.

STANDARD ABBREVIATIONS

Each programming manager may find it advantageous to develop a list of standard abbreviations. This will aid the reading of programs by other than the original programmer. Otherwise the following abbreviations

MSTR

MAST

MST

will all be used to abbreviate MASTER. Very simply, the use of standard abbreviations helps programmers understand old programs that must be modified. Using standard abbreviations and standard variable names is especially advantageous when many programmers are working on a large system.

For those who like to abbreviate in order to save keypunching, or must abbreviate because of variable name length restrictions, there is a set of rules available for abbreviating which will help maintain readability. These rules were developed by Michael Jackson in an excellent article in the April 1967 issue of *Datamation*. His rules for abbreviating are:

1. Abbreviate every significant word in the name, up to a maximum of three words.
2. Initial letters must always be present.
3. Consonants are more important than vowels.
4. The beginning of a word is more important than the end.
5. Abbreviate to between six and fifteen letters in all.

These rules are especially helpful to FORTRAN programmers because FORTRAN programmers are forced to abbreviate.

Keeping in mind the above rules, an algorithm for abbreviating is: The abbreviation within a word is formed by deleting vowels successively from the right-hand end of the word, until either all vowels have been deleted (except the initial letter of the word, if that is a vowel) or the word is reduced to the required size. If all vowels have been deleted and the word is still too large, the procedure is repeated, deleting consonants, until the required length is obtained.

Examples:

Names	Abbreviations
COST PLUS	CST PLS
ACCOUNTS RECEIVABLE	ACCNTS RECVBL
RECORD	RCRD
TRANSACTION	TRNSCTN

SPLITTING WORDS

Some programming languages allow the splitting of names or literals between two lines. It is never necessary to split a word and seldom necessary to split a literal. If a word cannot fit on the current line, begin the word on the next line. Although it may be permissible to split a word, the use of this option by the programmer tends to make the program more difficult to read and maintain.

If you are splitting a statement over two lines split after an operator. For example:

Careless form

```
A = B - C
  - (D + 2)
```

Better form

```
A = B - C -
  (D + 2)
```

The second example leaves a minus sign dangling on the first line which will immediately indicate to a reader that the statement is to be continued on the next line. In addition, if the second card should get lost in the first example a syntax error would not appear, but you would always get a syntax error in the second example if the second card was lost.

PUNCTUATION

Punctuation is another optional device in many languages. The most common optional unit is the comma. In COBOL, commas usually have no meaning and are often left out. For example:

COBOL

```
FD  CARD-IN
        RECORDING MODE IS F
        LABEL RECORDS ARE OMITTED
        RECORD CONTAINS 80 CHARACTERS
        DATA RECORD IS CARD-SALES.
```

This is a simple example of a COBOL coding where all optional commas are excluded. Here is the example with the commas placed at the end of each line.

```
FD  CARD-IN,
        RECORDING MODE IS F,
        LABEL RECORDS ARE OMITTED,
        RECORD CONTAINS 80 CHARACTERS,
        DATA RECORD IS CARD-SALES.
```

Predictably, the example with commas is easier to read. Each line is a complete thought and the comma indicates to the reader a temporary break in continuity. Another reason for using commas is to indicate that no period was accidentally left out. This helps eliminate one common source of error and makes checking for this type of error easier. Commas are cheap—confusion is expensive.

Another optional punctuation unit is the period in comments and output messages. Comments and messages are meant to be read, and the closer they are to normal usage the easier they are to read.

PLACEMENT OF STATEMENTS

Some programming languages allow several statements on one line; for example:

PL/I

```
X=A**3; IF A<B THEN GO TO FINISH; B=COS(C);
```

COBOL

```
FD  CARD-IN, RECORDING MODE IS F, LABEL RECORDS ARE
    OMITTED, RECORD CONTAINS 80 CHARACTERS, DATA RECORD IS CARD-SALES.
```

Multiple statements on one line are usually bad for two obvious reasons. First, it makes the program difficult to read; and second, it prevents other reading aids such as paragraphing.

A better approach is to place only one statement on each line.

PL/I

```
X = A**3;
IF A<B THEN GO TO FINISH;
B = COS(C);
```

COBOL

```
FD  CARD-IN
    RECORDING MODE IS F,
    LABEL RECORDS ARE OMITTED,
    RECORD CONTAINS 80 CHARACTERS
    DATA RECORD IS CARD-SALES.
```

This not only makes the program more readable but also facilitates the removal or modification of one statement without disturbing the other statements.

For example:

ALGOL W

```
A=14.2; FOR I:=1 UNTIL 10 DO BEGIN X(I):=0;K:=I*K;Y(I):=K,END;
```

Here is the same example with each statement on a new line:

ALGOL W

```
A := 14.2;
FOR I := 1 UNTIL 10 DO
  BEGIN
     X(I) := 0;
     K := I*K;
     Y(I) := K;
  END;
```

Maybe you noticed that the two above program segments are not the same. Can you find the error? If you do find the error, notice how many statements you will have to repunch in the first example in order to correct the error. Hint, for those of you who haven't found the error: it is in the first statement.

Another reason to place at most one statement on each line is that syntax error messages always indicate the line number. Thus, if only one statement is on each line, it is easier to locate the syntax error.

This suggestion also applies to headers such as paragraph headers or labels. By placing each paragraph header on a separate line it is not necessary to disturb the line containing the paragraph name for any later rewriting or rearrangement of the contents of that paragraph.

ALPHABETIZING LISTS

Programming languages are full of variable name lists, and the order of the lists is left up to the programmer. Two examples are lists of variable names which are having their precision or mode declared, and subroutine parameter lists.

The reason for alphabetizing the list is to make it easy to find a name in the list. Here, for example, are two lists:

FORTRAN

```
INTEGER BETA, Z, KEP, COST, PRICE, DOBT
REAL I, AMOUNT, SIZE, K, BETS
```

Now, if someone wants to find out if BETS is integer or real, he has to scan both lists completely. If the lists are extremely long, which they normally are in large programs, he may find this both time consuming and difficult. If the variable lists are alphabetized, however, the task becomes relatively simple.

```
INTEGER  BETA, COST, DOBT, KEP, PRICE, Z
REAL  AMOUNT, BETS, I, K, SIZE
```

Here are some of the commands that can use alphabetized lists:

FORTRAN	PL/I	COBOL	ALGOL W
INTEGER	DECLARE	File names	INTEGER
REAL	Parameter lists	Working storage variables	REAL
COMMON			LONG REAL
DIMENSION		Parameter lists	STRING
COMPLEX			LOGICAL
DOUBLE PRECISION			COMPLEX
Parameter lists			BITS
			Parameter lists

Alphabetizing can also be used in argument lists. For example:

```
CALL SUB1 (A, B, CTAX, X, Z)
```

Since the calling statement arguments must be matched with the subroutine or procedure parameter list, it isn't always possible to alphabetize the lists completely.

Another place where you can use alphabetizing is in the sequence of subroutines or procedures. Putting your subroutines in alphabetic order, whenever possible, will help you locate them faster. In FORTRAN, subroutines are separate programs, so alphabetizing is quite simple. In PL/I the procedures can easily be arranged alphabetically.

FORTRAN

If the statement numbers are in no sequence in large FORTRAN programs, it is quite difficult to find a statement number. And, since statement numbers are completely arbitrary, it is possible to renumber all the statement numbers once the program is debugged so the statement numbers are in sequence. A program can be provided to do this.

COBOL

Alphabetizing is not so easy in COBOL because the order of the paragraphs may affect the logic of the program. In order to maintain complete freedom of name choice, select regular mnemonic paragraph names, but add a sequence number. For example, if the paragraph names are

```
TEST-LOOP
RUN-ERROR
REPORT-OUT
```

then these paragraph names can be changed to indicate the relative location of that paragraph within the program by:

```
TEST-LOOP-600
RUN-ERROR-610
REPORT-OUT-620
```

The numbers used should allow for the inserting of new paragraphs.

In procedure oriented languages like PL/I, procedures are often nested within other procedures. In this case, alphabetizing the order of procedures is limited by the order of the nesting. One suggestion for helping to locate nested procedures is to use outer procedures as a prefix or suffix on the nested procedures. For example:

PL/I

```
SCAN:   PROCEDURE
          .
          .
          .
      SCAN_CHECK:   PROCEDURE
          .
          .
          .
```

```
            SCAN_CHECK TRACE:   PROCEDURE
                    .
                    .
                    .
            END SCAN_CHECK_TRACE;
            SCAN_CHECK_TRAP:   PROCEDURE
                    .
                    .
                    .
            END SCAN_CHECK_TRAP;
         END SCAN_CHECK;
         SCAN_DEBIT:   PROCEDURE
                    .
                    .
                    .
      END SCAN;
```

Since SCAN is the outer procedure, the programmer uses it as a prefix on the inner procedures.

Alphabetizing is one prerequisite for good readability. The second is neatness. That is, lists should be organized in columns. For example, note how difficult this is to read:

```
OCOMMON ALPHA,BETA,CHI,DELTA,EPSIL,ETA,GAMMA,IOTA,
1KAPPA,LAMBDA,MU,NU,OMEGA,OMICR,PHI,PI,PSI,RHO,
2SIGMA,TAU
```

compared to this form:

```
OCOMMON  ALPHA, BETA,  CHI,   DELTA,  EPSIL, ETA,
1        GAMMA, IOTA,  KAPPA, LAMBDA, MU,    NU,
2        OMEGA, OMICR, PHI,   PI,     PSI,   RHO,
```

Not many readers will disagree that the second example is easier to read than the first. In order to space column-wise, the programmer must allow enough room for the maximum number of characters used in variable names. Similar spacing should be used in all data lists, including input/output lists.

PARENTHESES

Parentheses properly used in programming greatly improve the readability of programs. Since mathematical and logical operations are governed by order of operation, programmers can quite often get by with few parentheses, but this makes reading and correcting a program much more difficult. The following examples illustrate this.

With few parentheses	*With extra parentheses*
`A*B*C/(D*E*F)`	`(A*B*C)/(D*E*F)`
`A*B/C*D/E*F`	`(A*B*D*F)/(C*E)`
`A**B**C`	`A**(B**C)`
`A/B/C/D`	`((A/B)/C)/D`
`A**B*C`	`(A**B)*C`
`X.GT.Y.OR.Q`	`(X.GT.Y).OR.Q`
`A+B.LT.C`	`(A+B).LT.C`

The basic rule is: when in doubt, over-parenthesize, not only to improve readability, but to prevent errors.

PARAGRAPHING

Paragraphing source programs is relatively new. Early computer languages such as FORTRAN or assembly languages were seldom paragraphed. Now, however, languages like PL/I or COBOL are usually paragraphed. There is even a trend toward paragraphing FORTRAN.

Paragraphing is the indenting of commands to indicate they belong together. While this does not affect the logic of the program, it greatly improves the readability. It is comparable to English writing practice, where a paragraph is a group of related sentences. Good paragraphing displays the logical structure of the program.

The first rule of paragraphing has to do with groups of statements bracketed by one of the following pairs:

FORTRAN

```
                    DO ... CONTINUE
```

ALGOL W

```
                    BEGIN ... END
```

PL/I

```
                    DO; ... END;
                    BEGIN; ... END;
                    PROCEDURE; ... END;
```

Loops are one common place where paragraphing can be used. The following are examples of loops which make use of paragraphing.

FORTRAN

```
      DO 10 I = 1, 16
         C = 0.0
         DO 8 K = 1, 12
            C =  C + B(K)
            D(K) = SQRT(K*1.0)
    8       CONTINUE
         A(I) = C
   10 CONTINUE
```

PL/I

```
      DO I = 1 to 16;
         C = 0.0;
         DO K = 1 TO 12;
            C = C + B(K);
            D(K) = SQRT(K);
         END;
         A(I) = C;
      END;
```

ALGOL W

```
      FOR I := 0 UNTIL 4 DO
         BEGIN
            X(I) := 0.0;
            B(I) := C(I);
         END;
```

In order to make absolutely clear to a reader of the program which two symbols form a pair, start both symbols in the same column. Statements enclosed by the pair are usually indented three spaces. These examples of nested loops show how paragraphing can help illustrate where loops start and end.

Loops are not the only place where paragraphing can be used. In most languages, paragraphing is used to illustrate grouping of commands.

PL/I

```
IF A<B THEN
   DO;
      C = A;
      A = B;
      B = C;
   END;
```

FORTRAN

```
   IF (A .LT. B) GO TO 16
      C = A
      A = B
      B = C
16 VAL = TAN(X)
```

The general rule is to put the IF statement on a line by itself, indenting all statements conditioned by it.

These examples illustrate which commands are grouped together by an IF statement. Similar grouping is possible with IF...THEN... ELSE commands.

PL/I

```
IF A<B THEN
      DO;
         A = -A;
         B = A*B;
      END;
   ELSE
      DO;
         A = A*B;
         B = -B;
      END;
```

Consistent indentation of 3 spaces is commonly used. This is enough
to indicate indentation and allows for several levels of indentation.
Another method of paragraphing with IF ... THEN ... ELSE is:

PL/I

```
IF A < B THEN
   DO;
      A = -A;
      B = A*B;
   END;
ELSE
   DO;
      A = A*B;
      B = -B;
   END;
```

I personally prefer the last method.

The OPEN/CLOSE statements of PL/I and COBOL can be paragraphed as follows:

COBOL

```
OPEN INPUT file-1,
           file-2,
     OUTPUT file-3.


CLOSE file-1,
      file-2,
      file-3.
```

PL/I

```
OPEN
   FILE(SYSIN)
         INPUT,
   FILE(SYSPRINT)
         OUTPUT;


CLOSE
   FILE(SYSIN)
   FILE(SYSPRINT);
```

Input/output statements can be likewise paragraphed:

COBOL

```
READ file-name
    AT END
        statement.
WRITE record-name
    BEFORE ADVANCING identifier LINES
        AT END-OF-PAGE
            statement.
```

PL/I

```
GET FILE (SYSIN)
    (PRICE, SALES_NUMBER);
PUT FILE (SYSPRINT) EDIT
    (TASK, NEW_RATE)
    (SKIP(2), COL(4), A, F(7) );
```

Complex IF statements that involve compound conditionals are easily read if they are paragraphed properly. One technique is to line up the IF, AND, OR, THEN, and ELSE.

COBOL

```
IF    (PARTS-NUMBER-PREFIX IN
      MASTER-HISTORY-FILE IS LESS THAN
          CURRENT-NUMBER-PREFIX,
OR    CURRENT-DATE IS EQUAL TO ZERO),
AND   CURRENT-COST IN DETAIL-INVOICE-FILE
          IS GREATER THAN 10.00
THEN
      (True commands)
ELSE
      (False commands).
```

In languages where variables are declared, the attributes should be lined up in straight columns to make reading easier.

COBOL

```
05 TOTAL-RECORD-COUNT  PICTURE 9(03)   VALUE ZERO.
05 FILLER              PICTURE X(04)   VALUE SPACES.
05 TOTAL-PAGE-COUNT    PICTURE 9(04).
05 FILLER              PICTURE X(23)   VALUE 'TOTAL COUNT OF RECORDS'.
```

PL/I

```
DECLARE  COST     FIXED(5)         INITIAL (0),
         TAXES    FIXED(5,2),
         HEADINGS CHARACTER(22)    INITIAL('TOTAL COUNT OF INSERTS');
```

In files, paragraphing should be used to indicate which items are subordinate items.

COBOL

```
01 NEW-PARTS-AREA.
   05  NEW-SEQUENCE-NUMBER     PICTURE 9(03).
   05  NEW-PAY-NUMBER.
       10  NEW-DEPT-CODE       PICTURE 9(02).
       10  NEW-EMPLOYEE-CODE   PICTURE 9(03).
   05  NEW-CHARGE-DEPT         PICTURE X(05).
```

A structure similar to paragraphing can be used with arithmetic statements. This structure is the lining up of all equal signs:

```
A    = B + C
SIGN = BASE*COUNT
COST = PAY + BONUS
```

This improves the neatness of the program and makes arithmetic statements more readable. Similarly, statements that exceed one line should have their turnlines indented so they align at right of the equal sign.

```
SIG = B*B + C/DES - COS(A) +
      PLAT/TEST
```

The above will fit in with the columnar placement better than the following:

```
SIG = B*B + C/DES - COS(A) +
PLAT/TEST
```

ALGOL W and PL/I allow procedures within procedures. In order to understand the structure of the program it is important that the nested procedures be carefully indicated. One method to indicate the nesting is by indenting nested procedures. Figure 1.2 is an example of this indenting.

SELECTION OF PARAGRAPH NAMES

Just as dividing a long essay into paragraphs makes reading easier, the dividing of the long program into paragraphs, sections, or subroutines improves readability by breaking up the program into logical units. This is also similar to breaking a book into chapters to avoid monotony and organize the material.

The names chosen for the sections should describe the intent of, or the processing activities involved in, the section. The use of sections also provides a convenient place for inserting comments. Place the comments at the beginning of each section, explaining the use of that section.

CONCLUSION

I hope I have shown that the small extra effort to make a program readable is minimal in comparison to the cost of revising, locating error, or rewriting an abstruse program. The rate of software production is about 10 fully checked-out machine instructions a day. At this cost, a little effort at readability can be quite profitable.

One mark of a good programmer is his ability to write readable programs. Anything else, in the long run, will be more costly both in programmer's time and computer time.

There are two reasons often given for badly written programs:

1. It is to be a "fast and dirty" program for limited use.
2. It is a crash project which is already late.

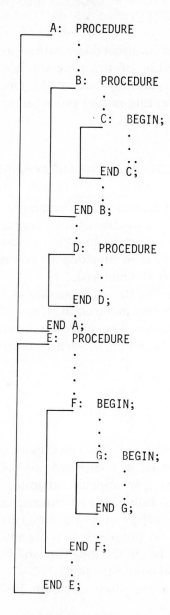

PL/I Paragraphing

Figure 1.2

But because programs have a tendency to stay around longer than planned and to grow in use far beyond the original plan, it seems worthwhile to write a good program the first time. Also, careful coding will save time in testing and revisions.

A great deal is said about the need for good documentation. If programs are readable, they become an important element in documentation. Another reason for demanding readable programs is that the program is the only part of the documentation that is guaranteed to be accurate and up-to-date. The idea behind readable source languages is that the documentation of the program is the program itself.

EXERCISES

1. Why should programs be readable?

2. How often should comments be inserted?

3. Name some obvious places to put comments.

4. Each program needs some general comments. What things should be included in these introductory comments?

5. How should variable names be chosen?

6. What rules can be used to produce readable abbreviations for variable names?

7. What considerations should be used in naming files?

8. What are the advantages of using standard abbreviations?

9. Where should blank lines be used?

10. Why is ample use of spaces desirable?

11. Why should an identification name be punched in program cards?

12. Why shouldn't you sequence number a program by units?

13. Does the language you program have any optional punctuation? Do you believe the optional punctuation should be used?

14. Why shouldn't multiple statements be placed on the same line?

15. In your programming language, where could alphabetized lists be used?

16. Find some examples in a program where parentheses will improve readability.

17. Modify one of your programs so paragraphing is used. Does it improve readability?

18. Can you think of any other generalized techniques to make programs more readable?

19. In your programming language is there a statement to cause an eject in the source listing?

20. What does the following program do? Criticize the program from a style viewpoint and then rewrite the program.

```
45   READ(5,32)X,Y
     IF(X.GT.40)GOTO10
32   FORMAT(2F8.2)
     GOTO21
10 R=Y*40+Y*1.5*(X-40)
 1 WRITE(6,32)R
   GOTO45
21 R=Y*X
   GOTO1
   END
```

21. What does the following code do?

FORTRAN

```
      DO 5 I = 1, N
        DO 5 J = 1, N
5           XMAT(I,J) = (I/J) * (J/I)
```

After you figure out what the above piece of code does, recode it in a clearer manner. Hint for non-FORTRAN programmers: I, J are integer variables which always result in integer results by truncation if necessary. Find three examples of tricky or cryptic coding and present them to the class for recoding.

22. If your programming language has no reserved words (i.e., FORTRAN, PL/I), write a small program using variable names that are usually used for commands. See if someone else can figure out what the program does.

23. If you can put multiple statements on one line in your programming language, write a program and use multiple statements for all lines. That is, jam as many statements as possible on each line before starting a new line. How difficult is the program to read and correct?

24. *Two excellent problems to program to test out the techniques in this and later chapters are Problem 25 (the 8-Queens problem) and Problem 36 (the ringworm problem) in Chapter VI. A solution for the 8-Queens problem is given in the paper by Niklaus Wirth, which is listed in the references in Chapter II.

25. Pick a problem out of Chapter VI.
    (a) Write the program in the worst possible style.
    (b) Write the same problem in the best possible style.
    (c) Try to use no GO TO's.

26. Write a program to read N, then read N numbers. Sort the numbers in ascending order and print the sorted numbers.

27. For I, J, K, and L positive integers less than 20, what integers satisfy the following relationship:

$$I^3 + J^3 + K^3 = L^3$$

28. Write a program to read the age of 100 individuals. Count the number of individuals in each block of 10 years. That is,

> years   0-9
> years 10-19
> years 20-29
>   etc.

Print the results of your counts in some readable fashion.

29. Write a program for the following number problems:
    (a) Use the digits 1 through 9 in different combinations and the operators plus and minus to obtain the total 100. You shouldn't need a computer to find some of these.

---

*The exercises work best if several people can do the same problem. Then compare the results and rank the programs according to style.

(b) Do (a) but restrict the solutions so the digits appear in ascending or descending order. Here are two examples:

$$123 + 4 - 5 + 67 - 89 = 100$$
$$9 - 8 + 76 - 5 + 4 + 3 + 21 = 100$$

(c) Do the same as (b) above, but use hexadecimal digits (123456789ABCDEF) to obtain the hexadecimal 100.

REFERENCES

De Biasi, Anthony J. "COBOL versus UnCOBOL," *Datamation.* June, 1968.

Flores, Ivan. "Intraprogram Documentation," *Data Processing Magazine.* Spring, 1972.

Jackson, Michael. "Mnemonics," *Datamation.* April, 1967.

Kreitzberg, Charles B., and Ben Shneiderman. *The Elements of FORTRAN Style*, 1972. New York: Harcourt Brace Jovanovich, Inc.

McCracken, Daniel D., and Gerald M. Weinberg. "How to Write a Readable FORTRAN Program," *Datamation.* October, 1972.

Maynard, Jeff. "Objectives of Program Design," *Software Age.* August/September, 1970.

Perry, Gerald L., and Jude T. Sommerfeld. "FORTRAN Programming Aids," *Software Age.* October/November, 1970.

Roberts, K. V. "The Readability of Computer Programs," *The Computer Bulletin.* March, 1967.

Simmons, Dick B. "The Art of Writing Large Programs," *Computer.* March/April, 1972.

Large monolithic programs are like a plate of spaghetti:
pull it here and something moves on the other side.

A good rule is to expect the worst at all times,
and program accordingly.

I don't program half as
good as I know how already.

II

Program Design

Program design permeates program style, efficiency, debugging, testing, and maintainability. Thus it is a very important part of any program development. But it is also an area where recommendations for one project or one programmer do not always work for a different project or programmer.

One obvious suggestion for better program design is: Design before coding. In the rush to get "something" started, the tendency is to start coding before the design stage is completed or sometimes even started.

Small programs do not offer the difficulty of large programs. Small programs can be easily coded and comprehended by one person. But how can we intellectually organize programs which are so large that they can't be comprehended by one person. Much work is being done on this problem, but at this time we are all amateurs when it comes to building *large* programs. Here are a few thoughts on program design.

THE SIMPLICITY GOAL

Simplicity in program design is the first step in writing a readable program. Coding should be simple. Sophisticated coding is not desirable, because complex logic or tricky coding can become very expensive when debugging or modifying needs to be done. Unusual coding (i.e., taking advantage of obscure machine-dependent capabilities) often impedes program checkout and certainly hinders future maintenance by programmers unfamiliar with the program.

Complex programs are sometimes written in an attempt to convince everyone that the programmer is indispensable. While this may be a valid goal from the programmer's viewpoint, it is not a valid goal from management's standpoint. Management's goal should be maximum clarity. Complex programs are worth their weight only in headaches and are an indication of bad programming. Complex or tricky programs are difficult for even the original programmer to debug or modify, and often prove an embarrassment to the original programmer when he is unable to get the program working correctly.

The structure of the program should make apparent sense. For example, if a test is performed that has several outcomes, it is most reasonable to list the code for each outcome in a sensible order, as by increasing magnitude of the test parameter. This method is most reasonable because a reader would expect it that way.

Another area where simplicity is of concern is in individual statements. During syntax checking the compiler could produce a message as follows:

SYNTAX ERROR AT LINE 37.

If line 37 is something like the following:

A = B/*C

then the error is easy to locate. But if the statement is quite long, or there are several statements on line 37, the error can be difficult to discover.

Another use of simple statements is when trying to locate an execution error after a line number is given. For example:

FIXED OVERFLOW AT LINE 56.

If the statement at line 56 is short the error is easier to pinpoint. But one should not go to the other extreme. For example:

$$ROOT1 = (-B + SQRT(B*B - 4*A*C)) / (2*A)$$

The above is easier to understand than the following:

```
BB = B*B
A1 = A*C
A2 = 4*A1
B1 = BB - A2
B2 = SQRT(B1)
BOTTOM = 2*A
TOP = -B + B2
ROOT1 = TOP/BOTTOM
```

The above is not only inefficient but prone to errors. It is also more difficult to understand.

The problem is: How do you decide what is a simple statement and what is a complex statement? This will vary by user and his familiarity with the programming language and the problem being programmed. One obvious guideline is that, in programming a numerical expression, the statement should not exceed one line.

Psychologists suggest that seven items are a good length to restrict statements. This is the same length as local telephone numbers, and seems to be a good limit to start at. Then each programmer can adjust the limit up or down, according to his own needs. In addition, each programmer will have to decide what an item is in a statement. As a programmer becomes more familiar with the language, it is usually natural to use longer statements.

Another way to improve simplicity in programs is to use consistency in coding techniques. This will help to reduce confusion. For example, all program switch variables should be used in the same manner. That is, a value zero (0) is used to mean "off" while a value unity (1) means "on." Likewise, it may be desirable to use the same table lookup method for all tables in one program. On input use, the same field width for all real data and the same field width for all integer data. This practice will eliminate many input errors. It is also best to avoid mixing real and integer data on the input data record when possible.

One method used at some installations to ensure simplicity in program design and coding is the *program buddy system*. The program buddy system consists of the rule that each program will be understood by at least two programmers. The first programmer does the coding, but a second programmer will be expected to understand and review the program.

A similar setup is the program standards evaluation. In this system a set of installation programming standards is established. Then each program is compared to these standards to ensure the standards are conformed to before the program is put in the program library. Usually all the programmers take turns doing the evaluating.

SELECTION OF ALGORITHM

The most important factor in having an efficient and correct program takes place before the program is written. It is the selection of the best algorithm for the program. This assumes that correct language has been chosen. Thus a good algorithm is a necessary, but not a sufficient, condition for a good program.

A very simple example of algorithm selection is the following equation:

$$Y = Ax^3 + Bx^2 + Cx + D$$

The most straightforward approach for finding the value of this equation would be:

```
Y = A*X**3 + B*X**2 + C*X + D
```

But repeated multiplication is more efficient than exponentiation for small integer powers so the equation should be changed to:

```
Y + A*X*X*X + B*X*X + C*X + D
```

Then this equation requires 6 multiplications and 3 additions. Now, to many people it might seem that this equation could not be improved since we have already improved it once. But even this simple problem can be greatly improved. For example (polynomial factoring—Horner's method):

$$
\begin{aligned}
Y &= Ax^3 + Bx^2 + Cx + D \\
&= D + Cx + Bx^2 + Ax^3 && \text{Reverse order.} \\
&= D + x(C + Bx + Ax^2) && \text{Factor an } x. \\
&= D + x(C + x(B + Ax)) && \text{Factor an } x.
\end{aligned}
$$

Now our equation would be:

$$
Y = D + X*(C + X*(B + A*X))
$$

This requires 3 multiplications and 3 additions. We have decreased the number of arithmetic operations. We have also increased the accuracy. This is called the "nested" form of the polynomial.

This example of improving an algorithm should help illustrate the rule that an hour of planning is usually worth five hours of programming. Too often all planning is skipped and the first algorithm thought of is programmed. Another example which is worth discussing is the problem of determining if a number N is a prime. A prime number is a number which is divisible only by 1 and itself. For example, 3, 5, 7, 11, 13, and 17 are primes. The numbers 4, 9, 21, and 35 are not primes. Figure 2.1 is one algorithm to find if N ($N > 2$) is prime.

This algorithm divides 2, 3, 4, ..., $n - 1$ into n until a number divides n exactly or until n is reached. This is not the most efficient way to determine if N is prime; however, it is an all too common first approach to the problem.

A simple bit of analysis would reveal that it is not necessary to check to see if all even numbers less than N are divisors. You need only check the number 2 because 2 will be a divisor if any other even number is a divisor. Then all that is needed is a test for divisibility by the odd integers 3, 5, 7, etc. This simple modification will reduce the calculations by about half. Armed with this new knowledge we can proceed to draw a new flowchart, as in Fig. 2.2.

This algorithm divides 2 and then the odd integers into n until a number divides n exactly or until n is reached. Most programmers,

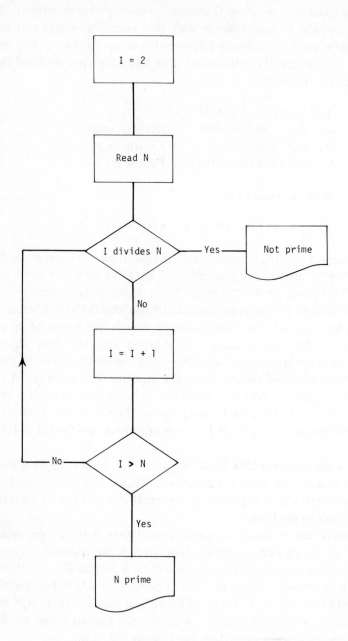

Figure 2.1. Algorithm 1

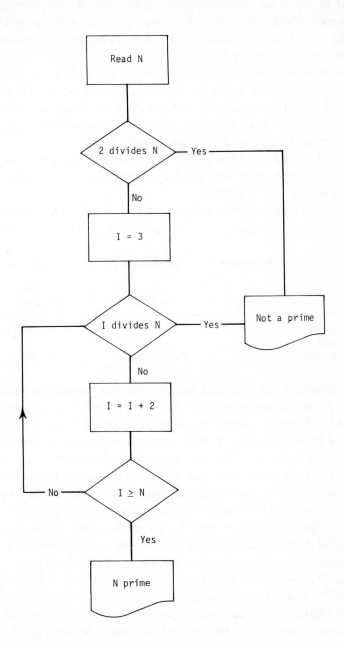

Figure 2.2. Algorithm 2

relieved at reducing their calculations by half, would start programming immediately. But since I am trying to stress the importance of carefully selecting your algorithm before starting to program, a little more analysis will be used.

The next step is to notice that all we must do is to test divisors that are less than or equal to the square root of N. (If there is a divisor larger than the square root of N there must be a divisor less than the square root of N.) If this is not immediately evident, try a few examples. So Fig. 2.3 is our new flowchart.

This algorithm divides 2 and then the odd integers less than or equal to the square root of n until a number divides n exactly or until the square root of n is reached.

Now let's examine the number of divisors we must check in each case in the three groups.

N	Algorithm 1 All I's	Algorithm 2 2 and Odd I's $< N$	Algorithm 3 2 and Odd I's $< \sqrt{N}$
10	8	5	2
100	98	50	5
1,000	998	500	50

By comparing the second and fourth columns we can see that twenty times as many numbers must be checked in method 1 as in method 3. From an efficiency viewpoint, selection of the correct algorithm is the most important step in this example and many other programs.

Now we have an efficient method to determine if a particular number is a prime number. But what was the original problem? Was it to determine if a particular number is prime, or was it to generate prime numbers? If it was the first, then we probably have a good algorithm. But if our goal was to generate prime numbers (that is, generate all primes less than 1,000) then we picked the wrong method completely. We could have used the Sieve of Eratosthenes.

This brings up the problem: "How does one select a good algorithm?" The first rule is: Don't immediately start programming the first algorithm thought of. You should at least consider several algorithms. Then choose the best of the ones considered. If you consider only one algorithm for solving the problem, it is usually doubtful that you will select the best algorithm.

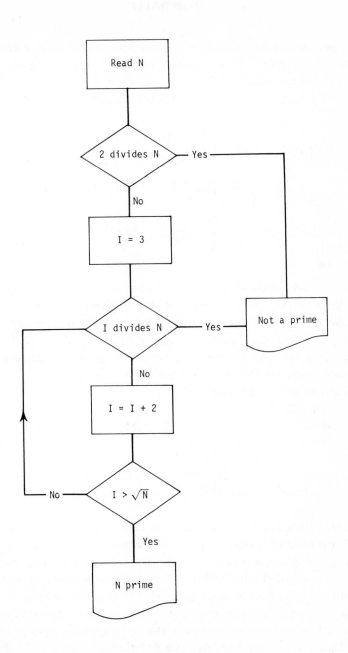

Figure 2.3. Algorithm 3

GENERALITY

Generality is the concept of program independence from a particular set of data. If a program is highly dependent on the data, then it is not general.

A very simple example of nongenerality is the following piece of code:

FORTRAN

```
READ (5,12)  (A(I), I=1,25)
SUM = 0.0
DO   20   I = 1,25
    SUM = SUM + A(I)
20 CONTINUE
```

The above reads in a vector A and sums the elements. But everything depends on the vector having 25 elements. If the program ever must be modified to handle some other number of elements than 25, one must search through the program changing each 25 to the new value. This approach is very prone to errors since it requires you to find *each* place where 25 is used for the vector A.

A much better approach is:

```
READ  (5,12)  (A(I), I=I,N)
SUM = 0.0
DO   20   I = 1,N
    SUM = SUM + A(I)
20   CONTINUE
```

Now, by changing the value of N we can handle any size vector from 1 to N (as long as N does not get too large).

A good general program will also handle the degenerate cases (that is, zero or 1) and print an error message when N is too large. Not only is the program then general, but it avoids errors.

Experienced programmers know that bringing generality into programs will save work later and make the program more robust. Always look for minor amendments or additions that will make a routine useful elsewhere. That way generalized subroutines can be contributed to a program library for use in other programs. Once a programmer or department starts this policy, a library of useful, tested subroutines is gradually built up. This will eliminate much dull and repetitious coding.

Another reason for writing general programs is that programs tend to require modifications. Generality can often anticipate many future changes in the program specifications. Also a careful examination for feasible generalizations may help clarify the design of the program. The search for generality can usually help anticipate future modifications and adaptations.

LIBRARIES

In order to improve program design, decrease debugging and testing, and thereby reduce the amount of work needed in programming, use program libraries which are already available. Plagiarism in programming is no sin. In fact, it is the smart way to do your programming.

The first type of library is the functions and subroutines available with the programming language. This includes all the standard functions such as square root, sine, cosine, absolute value, etc. Become familiar with supplied functions and subroutines by examining those in the programming language manual. Built-in functions supplied with the language are surely better programmed and tested than any we could write ourselves. So it would be wasteful to program a routine that was already available with the language.

The next source of functions and subroutines is your local installation. Most installations have some available—the only hitch is to determine what is available and how to use them.

Another source of library programs is books on programming and computer use. Quite a few books contain programs which are useful for library programs. Some effort should be made to become familiar with your own subject matter.

The final source of library programs is yourself. By programming in modules and keeping the principle of generality previously discussed in mind, you will slowly build up a source of useful subprograms.

STRUCTURED PROGRAMMING

One method suggested to produce better programs is structured programming. The goal of structured programming is to organize and discipline the program design and coding process in order to prevent most logic errors and to detect those remaining errors. Structured programming has two important characteristics:

1. Top-down design.
2. Modular design.

These two characteristics are discussed next.

Top-down Design

Top-down program design is similar to top-down report writing. Reports are structured hierarchically and written from the top of the hierarchy, that is, starting with a brief synopsis.

Thus the first thing to be done is to write a synopsis of what the program is supposed to be doing. Each module can have one sentence describing the action to take place. As soon as a module takes more than a line or a short paragraph to explain, redesign it.

Next, the data should be described, indicating the essential structures and the major processes to which the data will be subjected. This description should include carefully selected examples to illustrate the functions and their most important variations. These will be useful later as test cases. Each module should have the test data described when the module is described.

One major advantage of this method of working is that it guarantees that the documentation is produced. It should also lead to better programs. The programmer is forced to think about the structure, the data, and the testing of his program more carefully than otherwise in order to describe it on paper.

Much of the work on structured programming has suggested that program correctness is more likely simply because of the way the program is developed.

Coding. The first coding is best done with skeleton coding. Rather than aiming at finished code, the first steps should be aimed at exploring sizes of critical modules, and the complexity and adequacy of modules. Some of the critical modules should be further checked out.

The skeleton coding technique helps avoid the problem of large rewriting effort. For example, most large programs are modified extensively as they are coded and certain problems, restrictions, and desired changes become apparent. By doing a skeleton coding first, some of the problems may be discovered before a great deal of effort has been put into the programming.

Modular Design

In order for the structured programming to succeed, the program must be planned in a modular fashion. Modular programming is the dividing of your program into logical parts called modules, and the successive programming of each part. Once a large monolithic problem is divided into smaller logical, more workable units it is easier to understand and read.

Method of Coding. The segments of the program should be coded as follows. Write segments of code no longer than one page in length. Each segment should have only one entry at the top and one exit at the bottom. If other segments are called for within a segment, the other segments are likewise entered at the top and exited at the bottom, back into the calling segments.

The mainline routine should make all decisions governing the flow of data to proper processing routines. All common areas of storage should be defined as part of the mainline routine.

Next, within each segment there should be a minimum of paths. A very simple structure is preferred. Each routine should accomplish only one logical task. Each routine should perform all its own housekeeping to assume noninterference with other segments. In this way a processing routine will have tight logical control of its segment. No decision outside the segment should determine the processing within a segment; and likewise, no decision within a segment should determine the processing outside the segment.

Thus each routine is a closed routine. Control is transferred to the processing routine from the mainline routine, and when the routine has performed its function, it sends control back to the mainline routine. A processing routine can call another routine, but returns are always made to the calling routine.

In order to obtain a simple structure for each segment of the program GO TO statements are not used. Each segment should consist of straight line sequencing, with IF-THEN-ELSE, DO loops, CASE statements, or decision tables. Older languages such as FORTRAN or COBOL do not have enough language constructs so it is difficult to avoid use of all GO TO statements.

There are many advantages from a readability viewpoint when programmers use structured programming. A large program is broken into logical units similar to how a book is broken into chapters and the chapters into sections. Each logical segment is restricted to one page of code with a simple structure. This will help the reader comprehend what each segment does. There is one entry at the top and one exit at the bottom of the code. GO TO commands are not used in order to be able to read the code straight through without jumping around. Figure 2.4 is an example of a program that uses GO TO commands.

```
        GOTO: PROCEDURE OPTIONS (MAIN);

1               GOTO: PROCEDURE OPTIONS (MAIN);
        /*    A PROGRAM THAT USES TOO MANY GO TO'S.
                 WHAT DOES THE PROGRAM PRINT?
                                                    */
2                    K = 0;
3                    GO TO L4:
4           L2:  PUT LIST ('D'); GO TO L3;
6           L7:  PUT LIST ('E');  GO TO L5;
8           L4:  PUT LIST ('H');  GO TO L7;
10          L3:  PUT LIST ('O');  GO TO L1;
12          L5:  PUT LIST ('L');  K = K + 1;
14               IF K < 2 THEN GO TO L5;
16               GO TO L3;
17          L1:
        /*    DOES YOUR PROGRAM USE GO TO'S LIKE THIS?    */
        END GOTO;
```

Figure 2.4

Here are some of the commonly listed advantages of modular program design:

Conserve Main Memory. Infrequently used routines can be stored on a disk.

Programmer Efficiency. Common routines can be programmed in a generalized fashion and stored in a program library. Programmers can then use these routines as needed.

Computer Efficiency. Heavily used modules can be optimized to improve execution efficiency.

Easier Maintenance. If changes are necessary in a program made up of modules, the changes are usually localized within one or two modules. Furthermore, those parts of the program considered most likely to change can be assigned to separate modules at the beginning.

Discipline in Problem Solving. Modular program design forces the programmer to do a better job of program analysis. The analysis must identify each function that the program must perform and assign it to a module before allowing coding to begin.

Another very important advantage is easier debugging which is discussed in greater detail next.

Debugging

Modules reduce the effort needed to debug a program by limiting the scope of any bug. This is called *bulkheading*. Bulkheads are partitions used in ships to restrict fires or leaks to only one section. Likewise, modules restrict bugs to one section so they do not affect other sections of the program.

By keeping units small you will isolate bugs. It is much harder to find two interacting bugs than to locate two individual bugs. The smaller the program unit, the less chance there is of having two or more interacting bugs. Psychologically, when searching for errors we tend to search for one error instead of several interacting errors.

By breaking the program into modules we reduce the number of multiple errors, thus making debugging easier. But by breaking the program into modules we now introduce a new problem of checking out the interaction of the modules. This is an easier problem than trying to debug a large monolithic program since the interaction is reduced to the passing of the variables in the parameter list.

A small number of inputs is desirable. A commonly used limit is not more than seven input arguments. Modules that need large input lists should be further subdivided. The use of small argument lists instead of large common storage areas facilitates debugging since variables are controlled more tightly in an argument list.

The key to production success of any modular construct is a rigid specification of the interfaces. When debugging, you normally print input out to see if it is being read correctly. With a module the input is usually the variables passed to the module by the argument list or common storage. These variables should be printed from within the module while debugging to make sure all values are being inputted to the module correctly.

The most common error when working with modules is passing values incorrectly to a subroutine. It is possible to have an incorrect number of variables, pass them in the wrong mode, or write a long list out of order. The printing of the variables in the argument list inside the module should be one of the first things done.

The interactions of the modules have to be checked while debugging. Thus, output statements are needed to indicate when a module is entered and when it is exited. This will help provide a logic flow during debugging. It is best to write these output statements when originally writing the module since they will normally be necessary before debugging is complete.

REWRITING

Programmers should not be afraid to rewrite a program. Program writing is a creative task and, like other forms of composition, often requires more than one draft. When writing a program, it often becomes obvious that the first effort was done incorrectly. Thus, a rewriting will help produce a neat, efficient, and debuggable program.

One way to check for the need for rewriting is to adopt the buddy system. That is, each program must be understood by the original programmer and at least one other programmer. During program development both programmers would be expected to understand the program. This buddy system offers programming management a bonus in that if one of the programmers leaves, there is still available another programmer who understands the program.

EXERCISES

1. Why is it more difficult to program large programs than small programs?

2. Give some examples of simplicity and nonsimplicity in coding programs.

3. Do you think your programming would improve if you used the program buddy system?

4. Set up a list of good programming standards for your programming language.

5. What are some of the advantages of modular programming? What are some disadvantages?

6. Give some examples of generality and nongenerality in coding programs.

7. Take one of your own monolithic programs and modularize it.

8. Write the following programs with *very* many GO TO's and transfer statements: Read a set of numbers from individual cards. The last number of each card is -99. Then the program is to calculate the following:

SUM	The sum of the numbers on one card.
MAX	The maximum number on one card.
MIN	The minimum number on one card.
GLOBALSUM	The sum of all numbers read.
GLOBALMAX	The maximum of all numbers read.
GLOBALMIN	The minimum of all numbers read.

   Rewrite the program with as few GO TO's as possible. Which version is easier to read and debug?

9. Generate the first 1,000 prime numbers by using the first algorithm in this chapter, Fig. 2.1. Then improve the program as suggested and notice the difference in execution time.

10. If we wish to generate the first 1,000 prime numbers, we need to check only the previous prime numbers as factors. Why? Reprogram the prime number problem, using this knowledge. Can you improve on this method?

11. Program the prime number problem by using the following method: *Sieve of Eratosthenes*. Generate a list of positive integers from 1 to N. Start with 2 and delete all multiples of 2. The next number that has not been deleted is the next prime, which is 3. Starting with 3 delete all multiples of 3. The next nondeleted number is 5, which is the next prime. Delete all multiples of 5, etc. The list of numbers remaining will be the prime integers.

12. Write a detailed synopsis for the following program, then use it to write the program. The program is to read in integers and select the second largest value. The last number is a zero. Next generalize the problem: That is, select the Nth largest value where N is read in each time.

13. Write a detailed synopsis for the following problem: *Traveling Salesman*. The salesman has 16 cities in his territory. Since he buys his own gasoline, he always wishes to drive the shortest distance. Each Friday he is given a list of cities he has to cover the next week. He can visit the cities in any order and does not always visit all cities.

14. Write a detailed synopsis for the following problem. The synopsis should be clear enough so someone could use it to write a program. Indicate all modules and their interfaces. *Labyrinth and Minotaur*. Input is a 21 by 21 array of zeros (no path) and 1's (path). You are to write a program that reads the above array and finds a path. Your minotaur starts at the center of the array. If your minotaur is on a square, he can move to any of the 4 contiguous squares, provided they have a 1 in them. A zero is a blocked path. After you find a path out of the array, print the array indicating X in the path. Show only the direct path. That is, do not print backtracking.

15. Develop a synopsis for the following problem and program it. *Bank Deposit*. Interest is paid monthly at 6%. Deposits made by the 10th of the month receive interest for the whole month. In order to discourage people from making frequent withdrawals, anyone making more than 5 withdrawals in one month with a minimum balance of less than $1,000 is charged 50¢ a withdrawal for all withdrawals over 5. Interest is paid monthly on minimum balance during the month.

16. Write a program to print an exact copy of itself. No input statements are allowed.

17. Write a program to print a 100-character sequence of digits 0, 1, and 2 such that no two adjacent subsequences are identical. There is a solution to this problem in the book by Dahl listed in the references at the end of this chapter.

18. Simmons Factorial Conjecture. Only four factorials can be expressed as a product of three consecutive integers. Here are two:

$$4! = 2*3*4 = 24$$
$$5! = 4*5*6 = 120$$

Can you find two more? Can you find any more and prove the conjecture incorrect?

19. Program the following character string subroutines:
    (a) Write a subroutine that accepts integer numbers which have been read as a character string and convert them to integer values. Do the same for real numbers. Numbers can be positive or negative signed.
    (b) Write a subroutine that accepts an integer number and returns a character string with commas separating groups of three digits.

    $$1567842 \rightarrow 1,567,842$$

    Write a subroutine to reverse the process. Do all this for real numbers too.
    (c) Write a subroutine that does check protection. That is, the subroutine accepts a real number and returns a character string with a dollar sign and three asterisks in front of the number.

20. FORTRAN Programmers: Write a program to read a FORTRAN program and replace the old labels with labels which are in ascending order. Note you must not only change the labels in columns 1-5 but also change all labels on statements that reference the labels. This is not a trivial program to write. A similar program can be written for BASIC programmers.

21.   Write a program to find all the ways of cutting an $n \times n$ check-
      erboard into two equal parts (not counting rotations and re-
      flections). If n is odd, the center position is left out. Hint
      try a 4×4 first. Then add the restriction that the two pieces
      have to be identical in shape. Using the restriction, there are 15
      different ways on a 5×5.

REFERENCES

Buxton, J. N., and B. Randell. *Software Engineering Techniques.*
    NATO Science Committee 1969. Available from Scientific Af-
    fairs Division, NATO. Brussels 39, Belgium. $3.00

Dahl, O. J., Edsger W. Dijkstra, and C. A. R. Hoare. *Structured Pro-*
    gramming, 1972. New York: Academic Press.

Dijkstra, Edsger W. "GO TO Statement Considered Harmful," *Com-*
    munications of the ACM. March, 1968.

Maynard, Jeff. *Modular Programming*, 1972.   Philadelphia, Pa.
    Auerbach Publishers, Inc.

Maynard, Jeff.   "Objectives of Program Design," *Software Age.*
    August/September, 1970.

Mills, Harlen. "Top Down Programming in Large Systems" from
    Debugging Techniques in Large Systems. Englewood Cliffs, N. J.
    Prentice-Hall, Inc. 1971.

"Modular COBOL Programming," *EDP Analyser.* July, 1972.

Naur, Peter, and Brian Randell. *Software Engineering.* NATO Sci-
    ence Committee 1968. Available from Scientific Affairs Divi-
    sion, NATO. Brussels 39, Belgium. $3.00.

Wirth, Niklaus. "Program Development by Stepwise Refinement,"
    Communications of the ACM. April, 1971.

Why do we never have time to do it right,
but always plenty of time to do it over?

High efficiency reduces operating costs and makes things
possible that are impossible if the programs are inefficient.

III

Program Efficiency

Program efficiency is important at two stages of program development: at the compile stage and at the execution stage. If the compiler is too slow, a great amount of time will be used during compilation. If the execution of the program is slow, a great amount of time will be used during execution. But compilers that produce efficient object code tend to be large and slow because of work necessary to optimize object code.

Thus, there is a tendency towards using two compilers for each source language at the same installation. The first compiler is an extremely fast compiler, but it produces inefficient object code. This compiler is used during the debugging stage of program development. The second compiler is usually slower, but it produces efficient object code by optimizing the code. This compiler is used for producing object modules.

WATFIV is a very fast FORTRAN compiler which produces very good debug messages, but it produces relatively slow object code. WATBOL is a very fast COBOL debugging compiler. Both compilers are available from the University of Waterloo in Canada.

ALGOL W is a very fast ALGOL compiler which is available from Stanford University. There are several PL/I compilers available. PL/C is a very fast debugging compiler which is available from Cornell University. PL/I Optimizer is an optimizing compiler which is available from IBM.

But many installations have only one compiler for each language. Even then, correct selection of compiling options can reduce both compiling time and execution time. At the debug stage, assembly listing and object decks are usually not used, so these should not be supplied by default. Also, other options such as dumps, maps, and cross-reference lists are of no use if the programmer doesn't know how to use them or seldom uses them. A careful study of compiler options can result in either defaults or a recommended option list that can save considerable time.

Some of the compilers available today allow the user to select the resource which he wishes to optimize. That is, the user can either request that execution storage be minimized or that execution time be minimized. The optimization of one resource is done at the expense of the other.

Unfortunately, there is not a great deal that can be said about increasing the compiling speed. There are a few programming tricks that can reduce compiling time, but they are either trivial or extremely compiler-dependent. Techniques that work for one compiler do not affect a different compiler for the same machine.

Some compilers compile more efficiently if variable name lengths are evenly distributed. Other compilers compile more efficiently if statement labels are evenly distributed by the last character. Trivial techniques that will reduce compiling time for any compiler include eliminating unused labels and expressions. Labels prevent certain types of optimizations, so unused labels also prevent execution optimization. On re-runs, all source program errors should be corrected, and you should minimize the number of warning diagnostic messages whenever possible.

Some programmers consider concern for writing efficient programs archaic. But efficient programs run more cheaply, and cost is always important. If a program uses too much time or storage, the problem cannot be solved on a small machine. The last few years has seen a phenomenal growth in the use of the mini-computers so it is likely that the writing of efficient programs will continue to be important to the majority of computer users. Compilers for smaller machines do a poorer job of optimizing code than compilers for larger machines. Thus, the place where optimization is needed the worst is the place where it is available the least. If a larger optimizing compiler is available for larger versions of the same machine, it may pay to have production programs optimized at another installation if the programs will then execute faster at the original installation. Efficient coding means you can solve a great number of problems without having to resort to machine language or look for a larger computer — both of which are inconvenient.

A great deal can be said on how to make a program execute efficiently. The rest of the chapter is devoted to techniques that will produce programs that execute more efficiently.

The techniques described here are as machine-independent and language-independent as possible for optimizing the execution time and minimizing storage usage of compiled programs. The methods are machine-independent because the improvements made in the program will cause it to run faster on a variety of computers. They are relatively (except where specified for a particular language) language-independent in that they are applicable to high-level languages in general and the optimizing techniques do not depend on the characteristics of any particular language. Some of these suggestions on execution will produce more noticeable results on some machines than on others. Even different models of the same machine can have different assembly instruction sets that will provide noticeable differences of optimization.

Some compilers do optimization for program execution. Two types of optimizations are done:

1. Machine-dependent optimization.
2. Machine-independent optimization.

First, machine-dependent optimizations are totally dependent on the machine used. These optimizations are usually not generally known or understood by the source level programmer. These consist of methods of handling subscripts, register assignments, and analysis of machine instructions.

The second type of optimization is the machine-independent optimization that is done at the source language level. While the compiler can optimize a program, the programmer can usually optimize better, or at least help in the optimization. There are many optimizations that can be done only by the programmer since they require a knowledge of the logic of the program. Other compiler optimizations which could be done are not done simply because they would require too much machine time. Thus, the original programmer can do much to optimize his own program.

The use of the optimizing techniques discussed in this chapter does not eliminate the need for an optimizing compiler since the machine-dependent optimizing can seldom be anticipated or controlled at the source code level. Also, even the best optimized source program will be improved by an optimizing compiler.

EFFICIENCY VERSUS READABILITY

Most of the techniques that will make a program more efficient will not be detrimental to program readability. These techniques should be used as a matter of habit. But since I have attempted to make a thorough survey of efficient programming techniques for source programs, a few of the efficiency suggestions can be quite detrimental to providing a readable program.

My personal opinion is that completing a readable program is more important than an efficient program. This is because readable programs are easier to debug, modify, and maintain. And every major program must be revised, updated, or otherwise maintained by people other than the ones who originally wrote the program.

The extreme case is when the program *has* to be made more efficient. Either the program will not fit in core or it is taking too long to execute. Or the program is to be put in a library which will result in its heavy use. Then efficiency becomes very important and one must sacrifice readability for greater efficiency.

EXECUTION EFFICIENCY

Program efficiency during execution involves two resources. The first is the time the program will take to run, and the second is the storage it will require. Time has always been important to programmers since most programs are charged by the amount of machine time required. Since many computer installations now charge for the amounts of storage used, it is a good possibility that storage considerations will increase in importance; otherwise, storage only becomes important if not enough storage is available.

It is more difficult to optimize storage space than execution time. It is not unusual to optimize a program so it will run 25% faster, but it would be unusual to optimize a program and decrease storage space used by 25%. This assumes no serious blunders have been made in writing the original program.

Keep in mind, however, that if you should select a new and better algorithm and reprogram the problem, you might dramatically improve both execution time and storage space usage. The reason it is so difficult to reduce storage space use drastically, is that any savings are found in small amounts scattered throughout the program. By contrast, execution speed can be gained in large chunks simply by improving one section of code, such as a loop which is iterated numerous times.

But a small space saving is often needed desperately (to get the program to fit into the computer) while a small saving in time used is not very important.

You gain execution efficiency by doing as much as possible at compile time. This includes such things as initializing arrays and variables, calculations of constants, and storage allocations. Storage allocation at compile time usually increases storage usage at the expense of saving execution time.

Good programming practices will decrease both time and storage use, but some types of improvements in either one of these factors will often be detrimental to the other. Most of the techniques discussed in this chapter save both time and storage. If a technique causes a trade-off between time and storage, I'll mention it.

In most cases a small increase in efficiency is not worthwhile if it costs very much in programmer time, readability, generality, or convenience. But there are other cases when small increases in efficiency are worth a great deal of effort. One obvious example is in compilers where a great effort is expended to write very efficient programs. Since compilers are used over and over, a small increase in efficiency will pay large dividends. Another example where efficiency is important is in program libraries. Since these programs are used often, small increases in efficiency will usually repay the computer installation many times over.

The approach in each case depends on a number of factors such as cost of developing the program, how often the program is used, the relative speeds of different operations on the machine, and the way in which different statements are compiled.

A good program is a program that accomplishes the objective with a minimum of computer time. This is desirable because more jobs can be processed during a given time period. With the advent of multi-processing (that is, the processing of more than one job at the same time) the use of minimum storage is also desirable. This is because each program in a multi-processing environment must be allocated a region of core storage. The less core needed for each program, the more programs that can be kept in core at one time and thus processed at the same time. In a multi-processing environment core usage is as important as time usage, so charges are usually made for both resources. Reductions in either core usage or time usage will reduce program charges. Since computer resources are quite expensive, you will find that saving consistently even small amounts on a program that will be used repeatedly may be well worth the effort.

Usually any effort to improve efficiency is reserved for programs that are used often. While this is a productive approach, here is another approach that will also save you a great deal of computer time. Train yourself to develop a group of habits that will consistently provide you with more efficient programs. As a result you will always produce more efficient programs and consistently save machine time.

NONCONCERN FOR EFFICIENCY

Sometimes programs are used just a few times. In such cases the programmer is not concerned with program efficiency. Any large effort by the programmer to make his program more efficient would not be worth the work. Programs that are to be made efficient are usually programs that are to be used repeatedly over a long period of time.

Another situation where the programmer is not interested in efficiency occurs when the person programming is not a programmer. He may be a chemist, mathematician, or social scientist who is interested only in using the computer as a tool. Then his own time is usually the most valuable commodity, so no effort will be put into making the program efficient as long as the program will fit into the machine and run in a reasonable time. Thus, when writing the program some thought must be put into the question: "How efficient should the object code be?"

STORAGE

Usually no one worries about storage until he runs out. Then it becomes apparent that there is not infinite storage. The ideal situation is a fast machine with sufficient storage. This situation exists for only small jobs on large machines.

Shortage of computer storage is a very common problem. A few years ago it was thought that this would be a temporary problem since storage was becoming less expensive. It was predicted that soon there would be enough storage for any problem.

This prediction missed three important facts. First, the size of problems has increased as storage has increased. This fulfills the following rule: "The size of programming problems increases to fill the machine storage available for use." The second trend overlooked was the proliferation of the cheap mini-computers. Since mini-computers have become so common, the use of efficient programming has become very important. This is true both for storage and speed. And, finally, with the introduction of multiprocessing, no one program is allowed to occupy all of storage. Instead, core storage is divided into partitions of varying size. So if a program is compact enough to fit into an available smaller partition, the turn-around time is faster and cost less.

An increase in economical use of storage almost always causes an increase in programmer's time and execution time of the program. Thus, if storage is not charged for, storage usage is not of concern unless there is not enough of it.

Program Overlays

A program overlay is the technique for bringing routines into high-speed storage from some other form of storage during processing, so that several routines will occupy the same storage locations at different times. Overlays are used when the total storage requirements

for instructions exceed the available main storage. WATFIV FOR-
TRAN is one of the few systems that do not allow the use of
overlays.

The program must be broken into logical units so that nonover-
lapping units can serially be called into storage as needed. This approach is similar to breaking a large program into two or more programs. Program modules are usually used for overlays. Time is
necessary to transfer the modules from the peripheral storage device,
so execution time is used. Overlaying will conserve storage use, but
will cost extra programmer's time and machine time.

If a program might be overlayed, some thought must be put into
placement of data. Each time a new module is brought in from disk
storage it is a fresh module. No data are saved from the last use of
this module. For example, a module to produce headings might contain the page count, line counts, and special heading information. If
this module was overlayed, the accumulated data would be lost after
each overlay. The simplest solution to this problem is to remove all
working storage from the lower level modules and place it in the main
calling module. This calling module would never be overlayed.

It should be remembered that the use of overlays results in an
access to a disk each time an overlay segment is needed. This is
costly in execution time. Thus, only use overlays when absolutely
necessary. It is always better to check to see if the program size can
be reduced to avoid use of an overlay.

There are several general observations that can be made about
overlays to save both time and storage. Segments should be approximately the same size. Total memory requirements are influenced by
the largest overlay.

Do not "over segment." Each overlay costs a small amount of
nonoverlayable storage (segment dictionary), and a small amount of
additional code is needed to make the overlay calls. Also, overlays
take time. One should not execute a number of overlays for each
transaction. It is well to keep in mind that every call on an overlay
usually requires a disk read.

In order not to "over segment" it may be desirable to place
totally unrelated sections in the same segment to make the sizes fit
well. One first establishes the size of the largest segment, and then
checks to see if some of the smaller segments can be combined in
order to reduce overlay calls.

One can attempt to segment the programs in more than one way, and, using the same data, see how much time is saved or lost by a particular segmentation structure.

Virtual Memory

Another type of overlay is done by using virtual memory. If virtual memory is available on your computer, your program is automatically divided into fixed length segments (called pages) by the operating system. Then the operating system automatically transfers pages into main memory as needed. Thus, the problem of organizing an overlay vanishes from the programmer's purview and is assumed by the computer system.

The programmer has the illusion that he has a very large main memory at his disposal, even though the computer may have a relatively small memory. But time is lost when a section of the program is needed for execution and it is not available in main memory. It must then be read from a storage device. The less often this condition occurs the faster the program will execute.

There are two things the programmer can do to aid efficient execution when using virtual memory. The program should be written with subroutines. This aids *locality*, that is, the degree to which during execution a program favors some subset of its program. Locality is a readily observed phenomenon in programs. Two things that contribute to locality are loops and subroutines. Both will cause a program to execute repeatedly over a small set of the total program. The higher the degree of locality in a program using virtual memory, the more efficient the program will execute because it will not have to call as many pages into memory. Thus, when using virtual memory, keep things used with each other near each other.

The second method of increasing execution efficiency when using virtual memory is to group the subroutines together according to the order in which they are likely to call one another. This will tend to decrease the number of pages that must be read into main memory.

There are several classical examples of very simple programs that can degrade performance on virtual storage. Here is a FORTRAN program which zeros a double precision array:

```
        DO 15 K = 1, 512
          DO  15  L = 1, 20
 15           X(K,L) = 0.0
```

Unfortunately, arrays on the IBM FORTRAN compiler are stored by column and each column requires a 4K page. Thus each execution of line 15 will reference a different page. The inner loop will zero an element in 20 different pages and this will happen 512 times. The solution to this problem is just to reverse the order of the loop (that is, so the K = 1, 512 is the inner loop). Then the program will zero 512 elements in one page before requiring a new page. By making this simple change in the order of the loops we can decrease cost by 512 to one. Try running some similar programs on your virtual storage machine.

Report and Column Headings

Heading lines are often space-wasting items. The usual approach is to define the complete heading line as a literal. Another approach which saves storage when a majority of the heading is blank is to use code to accomplish the space fill. The cost is usually just a couple of instructions versus a large literal of blanks.

Heading routines are good routines to put in overlays since they are usually quite wasteful of storage and are not needed on every transaction. The literals for the headings should be "stored" in the overlay segment too.

Equivalence

Most computer languages have a command that allows two variables to share the same storage location. If a variable is used only in the beginning of a program and then a new variable is needed in another part of the program, these two variables can share the same storage locations since they are used at different times in the program.

This type of command can be used to conserve storage since it is common to have variables that are only used in segments of the program. The equivalencing of arrays can save large amounts of storage and should be carefully considered for a program needing more storage. A trivial technique for reducing storage is to reduce the size of arrays. This should be done before resorting to making two arrays equivalent in storage.

Using Loops

Use of loops for repeated operations is one common method to conserve storage. Sections of programs often have very similar sequences of operations. If the programmer wishes to conserve storage, he looks for similar sequences of coding that can be expressed in loops.

Loops require some extra storage because the initialization, the test procedure, the tally adjustment, and the constants must all be set up. But the reduction in total amount of storage is usually more than offset by the elimination of the duplicate instructions. Loops that are short but require an elaborate sequence of control operations can often be written by using straight-line coding rather than iterative coding. This is usually true only for very few iterations.

USING EFFICIENT COMMANDS

A limited amount of storage and time can be saved by using the most efficient commands. There are usually two ways to do many specific programming steps. Here are some pairs of commands that will normally both accomplish the same purpose.

FORTRAN

```
Logical IF
Arithmetic IF
```

PL/I

```
DO WHILE
DO I = ...
```

COBOL

```
COMPUTE
ADD
```

Experimentation is necessary to see which command uses the least storage.

Comparisons of two commands can be made by placing the command to be executed inside a loop and then executing the command a million times. This test is then repeated with the next command to be tested and then the two elapsed times are compared.

Another method of comparing commands is to see which command generates the most efficient code. The user can often determine a great deal by examining the assembly code generated for a particular command and comparing it to a similar command.

CALCULATION OF CONSTANTS

Programs are often more readable if expressions containing constants are used. But many compiler methods are used to do computations involving only constants. Some compilers will calculate all constant expressions at compile time and store the result. Other less sophisticated compilers store the constants and do the calculations at execution time. The latter method is very inefficient if constant expressions are within loops. Examples of constant expressions are:

```
TAX= INC - 3200/12
Y= SQRT(ABS(COS(2.30259 ** 1.839)))
INT=IRATE/365/12
B = 4.0 * A/3.0
```

All the above expressions have constants, but caution must be used where these expressions are inserted. If constant expressions are not evaluated at compile time, then constant expressions should always be placed outside loops.

This is commonly called *folding*: "the process of executing at compile-time source program operations whose values are known, so that they need not be executed at runtime." Folding is also done with values that can be determined within blocks of coding.

INITIALIZATION OF VARIABLES

Variables that are initialized when they are declared save execution time. This is because the variables are initialized during the compiling step instead of the execution step. Initializing of variables when declared aids documentation and helps avoid the error of not initializing a variable.

Most programs have some variables to be initialized. For example:

$$PI = 3.14159$$
$$E = 2.71828$$

Since these variables never change in value in the program they should be initialized in the declare statement.

PL/I

```
DECLARE (PI, E)
        REAL
        INITIAL (3.14159, 2.71828);
```

Two assignment statements are eliminated. This saves both storage and execution time.

ARITHMETIC OPERATIONS

Arithmetic operations are done at greatly different speeds. Thus, it is helpful to know which operations are faster because sometimes it is quite easy to substitute one operation for another. Here are the mathematical operations listed in order from fastest to slowest.

Fastest   1. Addition or subtraction
             2. Multiplication
             3. Division
Slowest   4. Exponentiation

Some fast mathematical operations are easily substituted for a slower operation.

Addition is faster than multiplication, so for multiplications with small integer powers, addition should be substituted. Thus $3 * I$ should be changed to $I + I + I$. If the expressions are not both integers, loss of accuracy can occur. The roundoff error with real numbers tends to accumulate instead of cancel. Thus, for R real and I integer, $I * R$ is more accurate than $R + R + R + \ldots$ (I times).

Rearrangement of equations can eliminate operations. For example, $X = 2*Y+(A-1)/P+2*T$ can be changed to $X = 2*(Y+T)+(A-1)/P$ which eliminates one multiplication.

Since division is slower, multiply whenever possible instead of dividing. For example, don't divide by five; multiply by 0.2 instead. Multiplication is usually at least twice as fast as division. Eliminate as many divisions as possible in your program and replace them with the reciprocal of the number.

$$\text{Not} \quad A/5.0 \qquad \text{Instead,} \quad A*0.2$$

If you continually divide by some number, say, X, in your calculations, replace it for its reciprocal.

Bad—X can be replaced by its reciprocal:

$$A = 1.0/X$$

$$.$$
$$.$$
$$.$$

$$C = B + D/X$$

Instead, use the reciprocal

$$RX = 1.0/X$$

$$.$$
$$.$$
$$.$$

$$A = RX$$

$$.$$
$$.$$
$$.$$

$$C = B + D*RX$$

This example substitutes one division for many divisions.

Another important consideration is the type of the power in exponentiation. Integers should be used whenever possible. For example:

Slow $A**8.0$ or $A**P$ where P is floating point
Faster $A**8$ or $A**I$ where I is an integer

Not only is the second method faster, it is more accurate and will eliminate certain types of errors since

$(-6)**I$ is allowed if I is an integer,
but $(-6)**P$ is usually not allowed,

because if P was 0.5, this would be the square root of a negative number. Thus, if you are using integer powers, make the exponent an integer form.

Slow $B = A**P$ where P is floating point
Faster $IP = P$
       $B = A**IP$ where IP is integer

When integers are used for exponents, the operation is performed by repeated multiplication. When floating point exponents are used, it is necessary to call a special subroutine to take care of the operation.

The function for square root is usually quite a bit faster and more accurate than using an exponent. That is,

Slow $A**0.5$
Faster $SQRT(A)$

Multiplication is much faster than exponentiation, so repeated multiplication should be used when the exponent is a small integer.

Slow $VOL = (4.0*R**3)/3.0$
Faster $VOL = (4.0*R*R*R)/3.0$

Exponentiation usually requires a library subprogram. Thus, repeated multiplication saves both core and time. Use the following when the exponent is a small integer exponent:

$X**2$ should be $X*X$
$X**3$ should be $X*X*X$
$X**4$ should be $(X*X)*(X*X)$

The last example contains a repeated calculation $(X*X)$ which can be further optimized. The substitution of one operation for a faster operation is called *reducing the strength of an operation.*

Reducing the strength of an operation, however, can sometimes reduce the readability of a program, so this fact should be considered. Also some machine time is used in handling intermediate results when reducing the strength of an operation.

Fixed-Point Arithmetic

Most computer languages allow integer arithmetic. Integer arithmetic can be used for any type of counting operation. Special arithmetic procedures for integers are used because many computing problems involve only integers (inventories, census information) and integer arithmetic is usually handled directly by a single machine instruction while floating-point arithmetic is performed by subroutines involving dozens of machine language instructions.

Some machines can execute 50 integer additions in the time required to execute one floating-point addition. In this case, integer arithmetic should be used whenever possible. This becomes especially true when a great number of simple integer arithmetic operations must be done, such as with subscripts. Using the wrong form of subscripts can drastically slow down any program.

A few machines actually do floating-point operations faster than fixed-point operations. These are generally huge scientific computers that have special hardware features to handle floating-point arithmetic operations.

Particular care must be taken so internal switches, counters, and variables that are involved in numerous calculations are defined in a form that results in the most efficient calculations. This is mainly a problem in PL/I and COBOL where it is possible to do arithmetic with variables that are really character strings. When this is done, numerous conversions are necessary for each calculation. Both storage and time can be saved by properly declaring the variables.

Mixed Data Types

Mixed data types result from the using of numbers that have different arithmetic attributes in arithmetic or logical operations. If you mix numbers that have different attributes, then conversions are often necessary to do the arithmetic. This situation can be lessened by declaring as many variables as possible to have the same attributes. Then less care must be taken to avoid mixing them since they all have the same attributes. Mixed arithmetic is allowed to cut down errors and help the programmer. But, mixed arithmetic should be avoided since it uses both extra time and storage.

Correct Mode

On some primitive compilers one must be careful about the type of constant used. For example:

$$A = 0 \qquad \text{Inefficient}$$
$$A = 0.0 \quad \text{Efficient}$$

Some compilers require a conversion from an integer zero to a real zero at execution time in the example $A = 0$ while in the second case no conversion is necessary. A good compiler stores the constant in the correct form at compile time instead of execution time.

If the conversion is necessary this can be very time consuming inside a loop. For example:

FORTRAN

```
DO 10  I = 1,1000
    A(I) = 0
10 CONTINUE
```

The above statements could cause 1,000 conversions. One should use

$$A(I) = 0.0$$

to avoid unnecessary conversions.

A similar situation arises from

$$Y = 1/X$$

which might necessitate a conversion where

$$Y = 1.0/X$$

would not cause a conversion. A simple method to avoid any problems is to write all constants in the dominant mode of the expression. Conversions of this type are usually necessary only on small compilers.

Decimal Alignment

Programs that use fixed decimal variables can be made more efficient by careful selection of variable attributes. If efficiency is important, then studying the language manual for your computer will be necessary for ascertaining when conversions are necessary in arithmetic operations.

Decimal points must be aligned in COBOL and PL/I, so a programmer should carefully select the attributes used with variables. For example:

COBOL

```
WORKING-STORAGE SECTION.
77 A   PICTURE S999V99.
77 B   PICTURE S99V9.
   .
   .
   .
PROCEDURE DIVISION.
   ADD A TO B.
```

Both time and internal storage can be saved by defining B as

```
77 B PICTURE S999V99.
```

This eliminates the extra instructions necessary to align the decimal point.

Grouping

When using a series of mixed mode operands that are separated by operators of equal priority, group the operands of like mode together with logically redundant parentheses. For example:

```
I Mode 1
A Mode 2
R Mode 3
I * A * I * R * A * R * I
```

should be written

$$((I * I * I) * A * A) * R * R$$

The grouping and parentheses help eliminate conversions that would otherwise have to take place.

Extra conversions can be avoided by converting from one mode to another once, and then using the mode needed. For example, if I and A are variables that are used together and they require extra conversions, then convert them once and use the correct form in all mathematical operations. For example:

```
Slow          B = A * I
              C = (A + I) * 2.0
              D = A * A/I
```

These statements use the variables A and I several times. It is better to convert I to A's mode once and then use the new variable. For example:

```
Faster        AI = I
              B = A * AI
              C = (A + AI) * 2.0
              D = A * A/AI
```

Now, I must be converted only once instead of three times.

Use Assembly Lists

One of the easiest ways to check the efficiency of different operations is to request a printing of the assembly code generated for each instruction. Then a casual examination of the number of assembly instructions generated for each higher level command will help demonstrate the relative efficiency of different methods of coding. Here is a program and its assembly listing.

FORTRAN

```
0008                      A = A+B
0009                      A = A+I
```

Assembly

```
000190 A = A + B 8      LE        0,100(0,13)       A
000194                  AF        0,104(0,13)       B
000198                  STE       0,100(0,13)       A
000190 A = A + I 9      L         0,108(0,13)       I
0001A0                  LPR       1,0
0001A2                  ST        1,156(0,13)
0001A6                  LD        0,152(0,13)
0001AA                  AD        0,136(0,13)
0001AE                  LTR       0,0
0001B0                  BALR      14,0
0001B2                  BC        11,6(0,14)
0001B6                  LCDR      0,0
0001B8                  AE        0,100(0,13)       A
0001BC                  STE       0,100(0,13)       A
```

The second addition requires a mode conversion.

Repeated Calculations

It may seem obvious not to repeat any operations, but repeated operations usually sneak into many parts of the program, especially loops. The best solution to this problem is to do as many of the simple calculations near the beginning of the program as possible, and then to use them as variables throughout the program. This is called *eliminating redundant* instructions. Some compilers do this for you.

Here are some examples of repeated operations:

```
Bad           X = Y + A/B*C
              Z = W + A/B*C
Instead       ABC = A/B*C
              X = Y + ABC
              Z = W + ABC
```

This points out another fact about efficiency. That is, the second group of statements is the longer, but it is most efficient and uses the least core. A smaller number of source statements does not prove that a program is more efficient time-wise or core-wise. In this example it is much cheaper to move A B C twice than to calculate A / B * C twice. Moves are very cheap.

Another example is:

Inefficient

```
SIGMA1 = SIN(THETA) + SIN(THETA) ** 2
SIGMA2 = SIN(THETA)/3.0
```

Efficient

```
RHO = SIN(THETA)
SIGMA1 = RHO + RHO * RHO
SIGMA2 = RHO/3.0
```

In this example, S I N must be computed only once, while in the first example it is calculated three times.

The natural method of solving a problem often introduces redundant expressions. For example, the normal method for finding the roots of a quadratic equation is:

```
ROOT1 = (-B + SQRT(B**2 - 4.0*A*C))/(2.0*A)
ROOT2 = (-B - SQRT(B**2 - 4.0*A*C))/(2.0*A)
```

But a more efficient (but less readable) coding is:

```
D = A + A
DIS = SQRT(B*B - 4.0*A*C)
ROOT1 = (-B + DIS)/D
ROOT2 = (-B - DIS)/D
```

The amount of time or storage saved varies, depending on the machine. On some machines a very simple repeated expression will save almost nothing by removing it. But the more complicated the repeated expression is, the greater is the saving. The saving also increases the more often the expression is used. On some small computers, floating-point operations are quite time consuming, especially if there is no floating-point hardware. Here there is the possibility of large savings.

FUNCTION CALLS

Some programs call many intrinsic functions such as SQRT, SIN, COS, ABS, etc. On some compilers one can have some control over how the functions are handled. If one wishes to reduce the execution time, it would be nice to have all functions end up as in-line code. If the goal is to reduce core usage, then it would be desirable to have just one copy of the code needed for the function and have function calls made to this copy.

An examination of the assembly code should indicate whether your compiler provides in-line code or function calls. If only one copy of the function code is desired, usually an EXTERNAL statement can be used to indicate that functions are not to be put in in-line code.

Function calls can be reduced by storing the values. There are usually many function calls in a program. If any of the function calls do not change arguments, then the values returned from the function should be saved to be used elsewhere in the program. Built-in functions like TIME or DATE are often used several places in the program, but DATE need never be called more than once in a program since its value can be saved.

COMPILER OPTIMIZATION

Some compilers do optimization which eliminates repeated calculations, but there are severe limitations on how much optimization is done. The greater the amount of optimization, the larger the compiler is and thus the slower the compiling. The programmer can at least help to optimize at the source language level. For example, compilers will not usually eliminate the following repeated expression:

$$A = X*Y + 2.0 + Y*X$$

Since the order is changed the compiler would not normally determine that $X*Y$ is the same as $Y*X$. Likewise, some compilers are not able to discover that $2.00*X$ is the same expression as $2.0*X$. Likewise, the following contains a hidden repeated expression:

$$A = B*B*C*C$$

If reordered, the repeated expression becomes obvious:

$$A = (B*C)*(B*C)$$

A different type of repeated expression is:

$$A = B - C$$
$$\cdot$$
$$\cdot$$
$$\cdot$$
$$D = C - B$$

The two expressions on the right side of the replacement sign are the same except for sign. These examples illustrate the many difficulties an optimizing compiler has in locating all repeated expressions. Thus the programmer should do his best to eliminate as many repeated expressions as possible.

Another limit on compiler optimization is that the compiler can optimize only linear sequence of code that has one entry (the first command executed) and one exit (the last command executed). This is called a *basic block*. Thus, the following group of code could be optimized.

PL/I

```
K = I/3.0*B;
P = 3 + I/3.0*B;
A = B*B + I/3.0*B;
```

The above statements must be entered at the first statement and exited at the last statement. But if a label is put on the second statement, the compiler can no longer optimize this code because it cannot determine the effect an entry at the second statement will have. For example:

PL/I

```
         K = I/3.0 + B;
LOOP1;   P = 3 + I/3.0*B;
         A = B*B + I/3.0*B;
```

The label LOOP1 prevents compiler optimization, but the programmer, by his superior knowledge of the logic of the program, knows whether these three statements can be optimized.

A similar situation is a nonstandard subroutine or function call that will prevent compiler optimization because the compiler cannot know which variables are changed in the subroutine.

AVOIDANCE OF LOOPS

When possible, avoid loops since time is spent in incrementing and testing the loop index. Subscripts can cause execution time to be increased by one third. Small calculations can often be done without loops.

For example, polynomial evaluation by

```
POLY = ((A(1)*X + A(2))*X + A(3))*X + A(4)
```

is faster than

FORTRAN

```
      POLY = A(1)
      DO 1    I = 2,4
    1 POLY = POLY*X + A(I)
```

In addition, the initializing features of each language should be used to initialize arrays. The commands that will initialize variables are:

Language	*Command*
FORTRAN	DATA
PL/I	INITIAL
COBOL	VALUE

These commands are the most efficient way to initialize a variable. These commands initialize variables during compilation instead of during execution.

One method of reducing loops is to collapse two or more loops into a single loop. Reduction of the number of loops is often possible by careful pre-programming analysis. Programs that have gone through extensive modification are especially susceptible to extra loops.

LOOP ORGANIZATION

When using loops, a great deal of time is spent in initializing and testing the loop index. Time can be saved by careful ordering of nested loops. For example:

PL/I

```
DO K = 1 TO 20;          loop initialization occurs 1 time
   DO J = 1 TO 10;       loop initialization occurs 20 times
      DO L = 1 TO 5;     loop initialization occurs 200 times
         .
         .
         .
      loop statements    useful statements occur 1,000 times
         .
         .
         .
      END;               loop closing occurs 1,000 times
   END;                  loop closing occurs 200 times
END;                     loop closing occurs 20 times
```

From the above statements, loop initialization occurs 221 times and loop closing occurs 1,220 times.

By rearranging the loops (this is not always possible) we can reduce the number of loop initializations and loop closings. For example:

PL/I

```
DO L = 1 TO 5;           loop initialization occurs 1 time
   DO J = 1 TO 10;       loop initialization occurs 5 times
      DO K = 1 TO 20;    loop initialization occurs 50 times
         .
         .
         .
      loop statements    useful statements occur 1,000 times
         .
         .
         .
      END;               loop closing occurs 1,000 times
   END;                  loop closing occurs 50 times
END;                     loop closing occurs 5 times
```

In this example there are 56 loop initializations and 1,055 loop closings. Thus, the number of loop initializations and loop closings can be reduced by nesting the loops so the outer loops have the least number of iterations.

LOOP OPTIMIZATION

When trying to make a program execute faster, loops are usually the most important. This is obvious since commands inside a loop may be executed many thousand times and any savings, no matter how small, will increase by a factor of thousands. One should make his whole program efficient by developing programming habits illustrated in this chapter. But if a programmer spends much time trying to improve the efficiency of his program by improving a statement which is only executed once, it is like trying to lose weight by trimming your fingernails—you might make a little progress, but it won't be very noticeable.

Thus, concentrate any extra effort in loops. Here is an example.

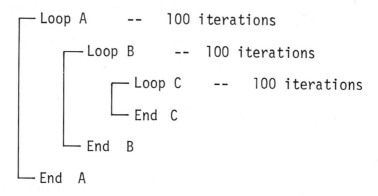

```
┌─ Loop  A      --     100 iterations
│     ┌─ Loop  B      --   100 iterations
│     │     ┌─ Loop  C    --    100 iterations
│     │     └─ End  C
│     └─ End   B
└─ End   A
```

First, concentrate on Loop C. Any savings, no matter how small, will be multiplied by $100 \times 100 \times 100 = 1,000,000$; that is, a factor of one million. A very small improvement inside Loop C would pay much higher dividends than a large improvement outside Loop C. Then concentrate on Loop B, and last, on Loop A.

The computation within a loop should be minimized. Thus, almost all the suggestions in this chapter should be applied to loops. This is especially true of repeated calculations, unchanged subscripts, arithmetic operations, and data conversions.

Repeated calculations are the most common efficiency errors in loops. For example:

```
┌─Loop  A

      ┌─Loop  B

            X  =  Y  *  Z  +  C(I,J)

      └─End    B

└─End    A
```

In this example Y*Z will be calculated every time the loop is executed, which may be thousands of times. Instead, the program should calculate Y*Z before the loop, as follows:

```
YZ  =  Y  *  Z

┌─Loop  A

      ┌─Loop  B

            X  =  YZ  +  C(I,J)

      └─End    B

└─End    A
```

Now the quantity Y*Z is calculated only once, no matter how many times the loop is executed. Significant results in saving computer time can usually be achieved simply by checking loops that do many iterations and eliminating repeated calculations inside these loops.

This is commonly referred to as removing *invariant* expressions from loops. Invariant expressions are expressions that are not changed within the loop. If at compile time we can remove a single multiplication out of a loop which iterated 1,000 times at execution time we can save 999 execution time multiplications. The removing of invariant expressions from loops incurs a small penalty in the necessary storage used for storing and retrieving the results of the expression.

This example of repeated calculations makes use of the subscript for part of the calculation. For example:

PL/I

```
DO I = 1 TO 10;
    DO J = 1 TO 10;
        A(I,J) = B(I,J) + D/I + D/K;
    END;
END;
```

The expressions D/K and D/I are repeated calculations and should be removed from the inner loop. For example:

PL/I

```
DK = D/K;
DO I = 1 TO 10;
    DI = D/I;
    DO J = 1 TO 10;
        A(I,J) = B(I,J) + DI + DK;
    END;
END;
```

In the above the calculation, D/K is done once instead of 100 times. Also the calculation D/L is done 10 times instead of 100 times. A move operation is substituted for a division operation. Moves are usually cheaper than arithmetic operations.

Some compilers do not process loop iterations as fast as expected because of costly loop-closing code. If this is true, the following may be improved:

FORTRAN

```
DO 12 I = 1,1000
    A(I) = 0.0
12 CONTINUE
```

An improvement may be made by the following:

FORTRAN
```
DO 12 I = 1,1000,2
   A(I) = 0.0
   A(I+1) = 0.0
12 CONTINUE
```

The above reduces the number of increments and loop closings by half. Notice that the above will require more core. This is called *unrolling* a loop.

Loops can often be combined. For example:

PL/I
```
DO I = 1 TO 500;
   X(I) = 0.0;
END;
DO I = 1 TO 500;
   Y(I) = 0.0;
END;
```

An obvious method to reduce both time and memory is:

```
DO I = 1 TO 500;
   X(I) = 0.0;
   Y(I) = 0.0;
END;
```

This is called *loop jamming*, or loop combining, or loop fusion. Loop jamming reduces loop overhead and reduces storage space usage.

A final example of loop optimization does the opposite of loop jamming:

ALGOL W
```
FOR I = 1 UNTIL 100
   DO
      IF (T) THEN X(I) = A(I) + B(I)
             ELSE X(I) = A(I) - B(I);
```

In the above statement, the IF statement must be evaluated for each iteration (100 times) even though the logical variable T cannot change within the loop. A more efficient method is:

ALGOL W

```
IF (T) THEN
        FOR I = 1 UNTIL 100 DO
            X(I) = A(I) + B(I)
        ELSE
        FOR I = 1 UNTIL 100 DO
            X(I) = A(I) - B(I);
```

Now, the IF statement is evaluated only once.   The above is called *unswitching*.   Execution time is decreased at the expense of core storage.

BRANCHING

From an efficiency viewpoint, branching is very wasteful. Also, from a readability standpoint, programs that are full of GO TO branches are usually very difficult to read and indicate poor design or a lot of program modification.

Thus, avoid branching whenever possible. For example:

COBOL

```
            MOVE 6 TO A.
            GO TO LOOPB.
    LOOPA.  COMPUTE A = 25 * C.
                     .
                     .
                     .
    LOOPB.  COMPUTE B = 6 * B.
```

In this program, since it always branches, why not change the order of the program to avoid the branch as follows?

COBOL

```
        MOVE 6 TO A.
        COMPUTE B = 6 * B.
                 .
                 .
                 .
        COMPUTE A = 25 * C.
```

The branch served no useful purpose and the reordering of the program eliminated the branch. Now, the logic of the program is also much easier to follow.

When using fall-through branches, make the next statement the most likely branch. For example:

PL/I

```
          IF A < 0.0 THEN GO TO LOOP1;
LOOP2:    A =   . . .
                .
                .
                .
LOOP1:    B =   . . .
```

In these statements, if A is less than 0.0, a branch will take place. The programmer should decide which of the two branches is most likely; that is, will A usually be less than zero or will it not? If A is usually less than zero, then the branch should be changed so the most likely occurrence will be next:

PL/I

```
          IF A ⩾ 0.0 THEN GO TO LOOP2;
LOOP1:    B =   . . .
                .
                .
                .
LOOP2:    A =   . . .
```

If the most likely occurrence follows this type of branch instruction, then a branch is eliminated most of the time.

On two- or three-way branches, the most likely branch should also follow the logical statement.

PL/I

```
          IF A = B THEN GO TO LOOP1
                   ELSE GO TO LOOP2;
LOOP3:    . . .
LOOP1:    . . .
LOOP2:    . . .
```

In this example, neither one of the branches follow the IF statement. Thus, the statements are poorly designed since one of the branches could follow the IF statement. This would eliminate a branch.

CONDITIONAL EXPRESSIONS

If the IF-THEN-ELSE construct is available, it can be used at some time during execution when a single variable must be checked for several values. The usual approach is the following:

```
IF A = 1 THEN MOVE C TO D.
IF A = 2 THEN MOVE C TO E.
IF A = 3 THEN MOVE D TO C.
            .
            .
            .
```

In the above statements, even if A = 1, all IF statements will be executed. By using the ELSE construct, the comparing can be terminated as soon as a TRUE condition is found. For example:

```
IF A = 1 THEN MOVE C TO D
    ELSE IF A = 2 THEN MOVE C TO E
            ELSE IF A = 3 THEN MOVE D TO C
            .
            .
            .
```

In the above statement, as soon as a TRUE condition is found the rest of the conditionals are skipped because of the ELSE.

A further improvement (which reduces readability) is to place the most likely condition to be TRUE first, and place the rest of the conditionals in order. That is, if A will usually have the value of 3, then that statement should be first.

```
IF A = 3 THEN MOVE D TO C
    ELSE  ...
```

One would also place the rest of the conditionals in order of their likelihood to be TRUE. This way the conditionals on an average will be completed as fast as possible.

Conditional expressions are often a source of repeated expressions. For example, if the roots of a quadratic equation are to be calculated, this is the formula:

$$\text{roots} = \frac{-b \pm \sqrt{b^2 - 4ac}}{2a}$$

The discriminant $(b^2 - 4ac)$ must be checked for a negative value since we cannot take the square root of a negative value. To program this we would probably do the following:

FORTRAN

```
      IF ( B*B - 4*A*C ) 25,10,10
10 ROOT1     (-B + SQRT(B*B - 4*A*C)) / (2*A)
      ROOT2 = ...
            .
            .
            .
```

The expression B * B - 4 * A * C is a repeated expression since it is used in the IF statement and in the solution for the roots. It would be better to calculate the expression before the IF statement and store the value as follows:

FORTRAN

```
      DIS = B*B - 4*A*C
      IF (DIS) 25,10,10
10 ROOT1 = (-B + SQRT(DIS)) / (2*A)
```

It is very easy to place complicated repeated expressions inside conditional statements since it is common to have to check part of the calculation first.

LOGICAL EXPRESSIONS

Proper ordering of logical expressions can save time at execution on an optimizing compiler. Some compilers will stop evaluating the following expressions as soon as the result is known:

```
A .OR. B .OR. ....
X .AND. Y .AND. Z ...
```

In the first expression, as soon as TRUE value is encountered the whole expression is true; while in the second expression, as soon as a FALSE value is encountered the complete expression is false. A good compiler stops evaluation as soon as the result is known. By proper selection of order of the variables in these expressions time can be saved at execution. That is, in the expression

```
A .OR. B .OR. C
```

the variable which is most likely to be true should be first. That is, if C is usually TRUE and A sometimes TRUE and B is seldom TRUE, then the order should be

```
C .OR. A .OR. B ...
```

To take advantage of evaluation optimization the programmer should arrange the variables in a left-to-right order so that the leftmost variable would most frequently cause termination of the entire logical expression.

Some compilers do not stop the evaluation as soon as the result is known. For example:

PL/I

```
IF A > B  &  C < D  THEN ...
```

The above expression can be rearranged to speed up execution as follows:

PL/I

```
IF A > B
   THEN IF C < D
            THEN ...
```

In the second example, it will not always be necessary to evaluate both comparisons.

SUBSCRIPTS

Subscripts are very costly, both in machine time and storage, but they also are very useful. Thus, no programmer would be willing to stop using subscripts, no matter what improvement in efficiency would be gained. But there are several things that can be done to improve the efficiency of subscripting.

If a subscripted item is referred to more than once within the same statement or group of statements, assign the element to a variable. For example:

$$X = (A(I) + 1/A(I)) + A(I)$$

should be changed to:

```
AI = A(I)
 X = (AI + 1/AI) + AI
```

The second example uses only one subscript evaluation, while the first needs three subscript evaluations.

Next, make sure you are not using subscripts inside loops where a single variable could be used. Here is an example of a nested loop:

PL/I

```
DO I = 1 TO 10;
  DO K = 1 TO 25;
     B(K) = B(K) + A(I);
  END;
END;
```

In this nested loop, A(I) must have its subscript calculated each pass through the inner loop, even though it does not change in the inner loop. A much more efficient program would be:

PL/I

```
DO   I = 1 TO 10;
     AI = A(I);
     DO K = 1 TO 25;
        B(K) = B(K) + AI;
     END;
END;
```

In the first program, the subscript for A (I) was calculated 25 × 10 = 250 times. In this second program the subscript for A (I) is calculated only 10 times. Since it is time consuming to calculate subscripts, you should remove all unnecessary subscripts from loops and replace them by unsubscripted variables. Figure 3.1 contains another example of reducing subscript calculations.

Another characteristic of subscripts is that the more subscripts, the less efficient the program. That is, an array of A(720) is much more efficient than an array of A(12, 5, 12). Most individuals would rather work with an array of two or more subscripts if this has mnemonic meaning to the programmer. But if the programmer has a subprogram that uses multiple subscripts, and the subprogram is heavily used, then a change to single subscripts is probably in order once the program is debugged. Some programmers use single dimensioning all the time and seem to feel there is little loss of readability.

To transform a two-dimensional N*M matrix into a vector of N*M elements, we can use one of the following:

A. When the first subscript is to vary the most rapidly the Kth element is given by:

$$\text{VECTOR (K) = MATRIX (I,J)}$$

where $K = I + [N*(J-1)]$

B. When the last subscript is to vary the most rapidly, the Kth element is given by:

$$\text{VECTOR (K) = MATRIX (I,J)}$$

where $K = J + [M*(I-1)]$

Method A changes $\begin{bmatrix} a & b & c \\ d & e & f \end{bmatrix}$ into $[a \quad d \quad b \quad e \quad c \quad f]$

Method B changes $\begin{bmatrix} a & b & c \\ d & e & f \end{bmatrix}$ into $[a \quad b \quad c \quad d \quad e \quad f]$

This method will reduce the readability of most programs, so it should be used sparingly.

PL/I   Slow

```
DO I = 1 TO N;
    DO J = 1 TO M;
        A(I,J) = 0;
        DO K = 1 TO L;
            A(I,J) = A(I,J) + B(J,K) * C(K,J);
        END;
    END;
END;
```

PL/I   Faster

```
DO I = 1 TO N;
    DO J = 1 TO M;
        TEMP = 0;
        DO K = 1 TO L;
            TEMP = TEMP + B(J,K) * C(K,J);
        END;
        A(I,J) = TEMP;
    END;
END;
```

Figure 3.1. An example of reducing subscript calculations

Another method for reducing the number of subscripts is to make two- or multi-dimensional arrays equivalent to a one-dimensional array. Very often it is necessary to set every element of a multi-dimensional array to zero. The normal method is:

FORTRAN

```
      DIMENSION A(2,3,4,5)
                 .
                 .
                 .
      DO 10 I = 1,2
        DO 10 J = 1,3
          DO 10 K = 1,4
            DO 10 L = 1,5
              A(I,J,K,L) = 0.0
   10 CONTINUE
                 .
                 .
                 .
```

The above requires 4 subscripts and 4 loops. A much more efficient solution to the same problem is:

FORTRAN

```
      DIMENSION A(2,3,4,5),B(120)
      EQUIVALENCE ( A(1,1,1,1),B(1) )
                 .
                 .
                 .
      DO 10 I = 1,120
        B(I) = 0.0
   10 CONTINUE
```

These statements set the four-dimensional array A equivalent to the one-dimensional array B. Then only one subscript and one loop are needed to zero the array. The above has the advantages of storage conservation, faster compile, and much faster execution. The disadvantage is it reduces readability of the program since a reader must notice that two arrays are equivalent. The reduction in readability can be a serious drawback if it contributes to confusion or makes modification of the program more difficult.

Complicated subscript calculations within a loop should be avoided. For example, in the statements

FORTRAN

```
    DO  6  I = 1, 10
        X(3*I+4) = Y(3*I+4) + C
6   CONTINUE
```

Two complicated subscript calculations are made each time the loop is executed. Since both subscripts are calculated the same, the subscript could be calculated once, set equal to a new variable, and then that variable used as follows:

FORTRAN

```
    DO  6  I=1, 10
        IK = 3*I+4
        X(IK) = Y(IK) + C
6   CONTINUE
```

Although this is an improvement, a greater improvement can be made by rewriting the loop incrementing:

FORTRAN

```
    DO  6  I = 7, 34, 3
        X(I) = Y(I) + C
6   CONTINUE
```

Subscripted-variables references with constant subscripts usually do not need any programmer optimization. Most compilers will calculate the address arithmetic during compilation for constant subscripts (such as $A(7) =$) so that no subscripting is necessary at execution.

Some languages such as PL/I allow array expressions. That is,

PL/I

```
    DO I = 1 to 100;
        A(I) = B(I)
    END;
```

can be replaced by

```
        A = B
```

The complete array will be processed if just the array name is mentioned. When you use array expressions, as in the example, the compiler will choose the most efficient method for handling the array.

Most compilers will input/output a whole array if just the array name (without a subscript) is listed in the I/O data list. This is the efficient way to I/O arrays, but it works only when the complete array is to be handled and when the order of array I/O is acceptable.

Subscript Mode

Every programming language has a special data type available for subscripting. This mode should be used whenever possible since it will speed up the subscripting. Use of the wrong mode for subscripts causes the machine to have to do several conversions for each subscript reference. The difference in efficiency is very easy to measure. Simply execute a program twice, once with inefficient subscripts and once with correct subscripts. The difference in execution time is usually quite noticeable. Subscripts are usually most efficient when in binary form.

Subscript Form

Most compilers permit a wide variety of arithmetic expressions as subscripts. But some constructions of subscript expressions permit optimizations. The constructions that permit optimizations are:

1. V integer variable
2. C integer constant
3. $V \pm C$ integer variable plus or minus an integer constant
4. $C*V$ positive integer constant times an integer variable
5. $C_1*V \pm C_2$ positive integer constant times integer variable plus or minus a positive integer constant

Some of the earlier compilers (FORTRAN II) actually restricted subscripts to the above form.

The subscripts must be exactly in the above forms. An algebraically equivalent subscript will usually not permit the same optimization. That is, $A(I+3)$ may permit optimization while $A(3+I)$ does not.

The above forms of subscripts permit at least partial evaluation at compile time. For example, $A(2)$ can have the location calculated at compile time so no subscript calculation is necessary during execution.

INPUT/OUTPUT

Input/Output (I/O) is very time consuming and should always be cut to a minimum. This means: Do not read anything in that can be calculated inside the program. In addition, make sure that each I/O statement transfers as much information as possible to or from a minimum of physical records. That is, two consecutive I/O commands to the same device can often be combined into one command. This reduces the number of calls to the general I/O subroutines and supervisory requests. Also, don't forget after debugging to remove all excess I/O statements.

Each language has a most efficient way to read or write information. If a program is doing a lot of input or output, considerable time can usually be saved by using the most efficient method of I/O. For example, unformatted I/O is usually faster than formatted I/O. Unformatted I/O can be used with tapes, disks, and cards if the data is to be written out and then reread by the same or a different program. Accuracy is also better with unformatted records, and less space is needed. Unformatted I/O is faster because it requires no conversions or formatting of data from internal to external form, or vice versa. Unformatted I/O is more accurate because significant digits can be dropped when converting data from the internal machined form to the external formatted form.

Printed Output

Printed output should be reduced to the minimum necessary. Not only is it time consuming to print, but large reports full of pages of numbers are seldom read by anyone. Instead, print only what the user wishes to read. Apart from saving machine time, paper, and money, the computer can disregard all uninteresting results (which have to be adequately specified) far more quickly than unwanted paper can be torn up and assigned to the waste basket. From an efficiency viewpoint it is almost always cheaper to write the extra statements to eliminate unwanted output than to print out unwanted output.

Computer paper is expensive, so don't print just one number on a line when printing many lines. Program ecologically—print as much information as readable on each line. Old computer printouts can be used as scratch paper. Also, computer cards and paper are high grade material which can be profitably recycled.

Cards

When using cards, read or punch as few as possible. This is achieved by packing as much information as possible on each card. Decimals can usually be eliminated, which means more digits can be placed on one card.

But the format of information on the card is limited by the input source or what other uses the card is to be put to. If the physical card is not needed and volume is large, then tape or disk files should always be considered in place of cards.

Sometimes input can be greatly reduced. Here is a column of numbers that could be input:

$$
\begin{array}{l}
10.0 \\
10.1 \\
10.2 \\
\;\;\;\bullet \\
\;\;\;\bullet \\
\;\;\;\bullet \\
24.9 \\
25.0
\end{array}
$$

This approach wastes a great deal of machine time since you could read the starting and ending value $(10.0, 25.0)$, and the increment (0.1), and the computer can calculate the intervening values.

Magnetic Tapes

If you are storing intermediate computer data that does not require physical form, such as cards, then magnetic tape is usually cheaper. Magnetic tape can be used only for sequential files. A comparison of the cost of magnetic tapes and cards shows that as soon as you wish to punch over 10,000 cards, a magnetic tape is cheaper. This, however, is only half the picture since magnetic tape can be used over and over and cards can be used only once. And cards are very bulky while magnetic tape is compact. The only time cards should be used for output is when the volume is very small, say, less than 2,000 cards, or when the physical card is needed for some other purpose.

A tape is much more efficient in storing data or processing data. The slowest tape drives can write about 4,000 characters per *second* while the fastest card punches can punch only 80,000 characters per *minute*. A magnetic tape can easily hold 200,000 cards.

Tapes can be used efficiently or inefficiently, depending on how the data is organized on the tape. Tapes are organized into records, blocks, and files. A *file* is the complete set of records processed in the job. A *block* is a collection of records. And the *record* is the data that is processed each time a read or write command appears in the program. If records are unblocked, then each time a record is read it is read from the tape. Reading the physical tape is slow and inefficient in comparison to reading from a buffer area. If records are grouped into blocks, then the whole block is read and stored in a buffer at one time. Each write command in the program then puts a record in the buffer area. Once the buffer is full, a physical write (issued by the control program) records the block on the tape. Input works similarly; that is, blocks of records are read automatically from the tape, and each input statement of the program causes one record to be transferred from the buffer. The computer can transfer records from the buffer much faster than from the tape.

Here is how a block of records looks on a tape.

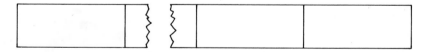

This block has *n* records. When the block is exhausted a new block is read in automatically by the supervisor. Usually, input/output is double-buffered, which means two blocks are available. Thus blocks of records can be transferred to or from one buffer while the other buffer is being processed. The collection of records into a buffer area and transfer of a block of records from or to the magnetic tape are handled automatically by the computer. All the programmer does is specify the record type, record size, and buffer size. If blocks are large enough, there should be no waiting for input/output since one buffer should always be ready for use.

Each block is separated by inter-block gap (IBG) which requires six-tenths of an inch of tape. This is required by the tape drives for proper reading. If you put unblocked card images on a tape with a recording density of 800 bpi (bytes per inch) this means that 80 characters would need 0.1 inch. Since the IBG needs 0.6 inch, Fig. 3.2 shows how the tape would look. Thus, the ratio of IBG to data is 6:1, which means a great deal of time is spent reading the IBG. In contrast, if blocks are 1,600 characters long (20 card images), there is only one 0.6 inch IBG for each 2.0 inches of data.

0.6 inch ±BG

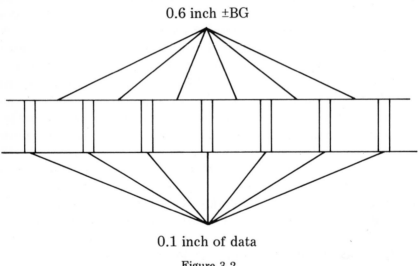

0.1 inch of data

Figure 3.2

Efficiency is gained by using large blocks in sequential files. If only one record is in each block, this means a block must be processed for each input/output statement. Since it is common to charge for input/output (I/O), this can be quite expensive. Also, much time is wasted while waiting for new records to be processed. If ten records are included in each block, only 1/10 as many I/O must be done. And if 100 records are to be included in each block, only 1/100 as many I/O's must be done. This may lead the unexpecting to assume that very large blocks are then always best, which is partially true.

There are two problems that prevent using infinite blocks: errors and storage. If you have an input/output error on a tape, you will often lose the whole block. If this is one record, then the loss is not as serious as losing a block of 1,000 records. So if tape I/O errors are common, use small blocks. But most tape I/O errors are caused by dirty tape drives, so it would be better to start keeping your tape drives cleaner.

Buffers

The second limitation is storage requirements. This is a case where execution efficiency costs storage. The larger your block size, the less time needed and the more storage needed. Each buffer requires storage. There is usually a maximum-size block which can be read. On some computers this is 32,760 characters. If there are two buffers and your block size is the maximum, which may be 32,760 characters, then the buffers use 65,520 characters of storage. If your program is large or your computer size is small, then this block size would not be possible.

Thus, what is an easy answer? Assuming that I/O errors are not much of a problem (and they shouldn't be if the tape drives are clean and maintenance is good), then a block size of 4,000 characters would normally be a minimum. This would be 50 card images (50 × 80 = 4,000). Maximum would be what could be handled by storage.

In order to optimize the tape handling so as not to have blocks too small or too large, an ideal situation is the following. Each time a block of data is processing, some computing is done. That is, some calculations are done on the block. Thus, ideally we always want a block of data waiting for computing. The computer can process a buffer while other computing is going on. So, if the amount of time necessary to do the computations on each block was just a little greater than the amount of time needed to I/O an old block, then, on a double buffer machine, a block of data would always be available. Also, block sizes would not have to be excessively large.*

Thus, on a file where each record involves a great deal of calculation, small block sizes can be used. But on an inactive file or where little calculation is done, longer block sizes should increase efficiency.

*Appendix III contains an article on selecting mathematically correct blocking factors.

Some machines allow for an increase in the number of buffers. For long jobs that have a great deal of input/output, one might compare the execution times for a few test runs using different numbers of buffers and different size blocks in order to determine the most efficient combination.

The number of buffers to assign to each file can be established for each program. But since buffers require storage there is often a limit to the number of buffers used. One major method to save buffer space is to have more than one buffer use the same storage. This is only possible when two or more files will not be open at the same time. This will allow one file to use a buffer area early in a program and allow another to use the same buffer area after the first file has been closed.

It is common in programming for one file to be used by several programs. We can adjust the number of buffers used for each program, but we cannot change the blocking factor for most file types (that is, for sequential tape files) for each program since the record size and blocking factor are already established. Therefore, the system design phase must carefully consider block size in respect to memory requirements and speed of processing for each job in the system. Otherwise, too much storage will be used or processing might be quite slow.

Most systems are double buffered. That is, there are two buffers assigned to each file. If storage is desperately needed, one should remember the second buffer. This second buffer can usually be eliminated, which will result in a savings in storage and cost execution time because there will be no overlapping of I/O operations.

Disk Files

It is more difficult to state how to organize disk files for efficient processing than tape because there are many ways to organize disk files. But a few important principles can be stated.

First, unformatted I/O should be used with disk files. Efficiency is improved in two ways: There is a space savings of disk space, and no conversion from internal (machine) data to an external (disk) representation is needed. Furthermore, unformatted I/O always provides the best accuracy in transferring data.

When using more than one disk file in the same job, do not place all the files on the same disk. Instead, place the files on different disks in order to allow overlapping of file processing. If two files are placed on the same disk, too much time is lost waiting for the disk arm to be correctly positioned. If possible, make sure that the disk files use different channels, too.

Sequential Files. For sequential disk files the blocks of data should be close to, but not exceed, the capacity of a track. This is 3,625 bytes on an IBM 2311 disk. If the program is so large that blocks of this size cannot be accommodated within the computer, an integral number of blocks should be fitted to a track. Disk space is needed for inter-block gaps; so the smaller the blocks, the more disk space is used for the IBG. Efficient sizes for such blocks are 3,625, 1,740, 1,131, 830, 651. The block size should be as close as possible to (but not larger than) one of these sizes.

Thus, sequential disk files are similar to sequential tape files in that larger blocks (but not greater than the track capacity) provide the most efficient operation. Transfer of many very short logical blocks is undesirable.

If the processing is I/O bound, it may be more efficient to decrease the size of the block and increase the number of buffers used. Long jobs can try some experimentation, using different combinations of block size and number of buffers to determine the most efficient combinations.

EXPLORE NEW COMMANDS

Once a programmer has achieved a reasonable familiarity with his programming language, he should read the programming reference manual in detail. While reading the reference manual, try using some of the program language commands that you have not used in the past. Then you will probably discover that you have not been using many commands to their fullest capacity.

A re-reading of the reference manual will introduce fresh programming techniques, and hopefully some of them will result in more efficient programs.

WARNING MESSAGES

An often overlooked technique for drastic improvement of compiling and executing efficiency is removal of any conditions causing warning messages. Since warning messages do not prevent execution of the program, there is a tendency to ignore them. This is a very serious error from an efficiency viewpoint. Time is lost each time a compile is done, and severe penalties of execution time or core usage can result.

In FORTRAN, for example, variables used in COMMON statements must be aligned properly. If they are not aligned, *considerable* execution time can be lost.

The correction of any code to remove warning messages at compile time is probably the easiest and most profitable method to increase execution efficiency. Thus, programmers interested in efficient execution should first check to see if they can remove any compile warning messages. Warning messages are often given on alignment problems and conversions.

OBJECT MODULES

Object modules are compiled programs. Object modules should be used for all production programs. Once a program is debugged and tested, an object module can be created for future runs. Object modules can be in the form of object card decks, object modules on tape, or object modules on disk. The object modules on disk are the most efficient. Object modules save time by eliminating the compiling step each time the program is executed. Recompiling a source deck for each production run is very wasteful and usually not necessary.

MODULES

Since the aim of this chapter is to cover program efficiency in full, I will list one of the main efficiency disadvantages of using modules. But my personal belief is that the multitude of advantages (readability, maintainability, debugging, testing) of modular approach outweigh any disadvantages of less efficient program execution.

Modular design aids writing, debugging, testing, and modification and thus can save a great amount of programming time and machine time at the writing stage. Since some programs spend more machine time at the writing stage than the production stage, this is an important consideration.

Subroutines can be programmed, debugged, and tested individually. This means machine time can be saved because long programs increase in compiling time faster than linearly.

A disadvantage when using subroutines is that subroutines can cost core storage. Subroutines cost storage and time because linkage instructions are necessary to coordinate the calling program with its subroutines. Some COBOL compilers require a fixed overhead of 1K core for each subroutine. But the space penalty is easily made up if the subroutine is called from more than one place in the main program, since otherwise the subroutine would have to appear in several places.

Strictly from an efficiency viewpoint, a subroutine that is called from only one place in the main program could be handled more efficiently by being coded at the place called from instead of using a subroutine. Coding in line eliminates the linkage instructions and thus saves time and storage.

You must decide if your primary interest is saving time or storage since this is a situation where saving of one resource results in using the other resource. If the primary interest is in saving execution time, then subroutines should not be used and the coding should be done in line. But if the primary consideration is saving storage space, then tasks that would appear more than once in the program should be considered for subroutines.

If the subroutine must pass an argument list, extra time and storage are needed. Argument addresses must be passed from the calling main program and then linked in some fashion to the instructions that will use them. All this takes time and storage.

If the argument list can be eliminated or reduced, considerable savings can take place. The normal method for reducing or eliminating argument lists is to use the command that places these variables in a common storage area where all the subprograms can find the variables.

Therefore, when a variable in a subroutine always corresponds to the same variable in the main program at every call of the subroutine, the variable should be placed in the common area. But when a variable in the subroutine may correspond to different variables at different calls from the main program, the variable must be part of the argument list. If an argument is normally a constant, it can be assigned to a variable that can then be placed in common. There is a tendency to place all variables in an argument list. This should be avoided since the common storage is much more efficient. Both storage and time are saved by using common storage.

Another method to reduce the number of items in a parameter list is to combine several to form a contiguous area. For example, a module for doing heading routines may have a number of items passed as parameters, such as date, page count, heading labels, etc. If these items are combined into a single data area, the number of parameters can be reduced. Languages such as PL/I and COBOL have data structures available that make it easy to combine items into one data item.

On some compilers, if a variable is in the argument list, extra instructions are needed to use any argument variable. For example:

FORTRAN

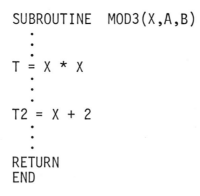

```
SUBROUTINE  MOD3(X,A,B)
         .
         .
         .
T = X * X
         .
         .
         .
T2 = X + 2
         .
         .
         .
RETURN
END
```

In this program, variable X is used three times, and the linking instructions to locate the variable X will be needed three times.

Savings in both storage and execution time can be achieved by assigning the argument variable to a variable inside the subroutine as follows:

FORTRAN

```
SUBROUTINE  MOD3 (X,A,B)
XX = X
  .
  .
  .
T = XX * XX
  .
  .
  .
T2 = XX + 2
  .
  .
RETURN
END
```

Modules increase the recompilation efficiency. If modules are not used and one error is discovered in a large monolithic program, the whole program must be recompiled. The *recompilation efficiency* is very low, that is, the number of statements that are changed as compared with the number of statements that must be recompiled. Thus, on large monolithic programs, we find an error, recompile the whole program, find a new error, recompile the whole program, etc. If modules are used, even if we do not find the error until the modules have been put together, we will often have to recompile only one module.

OPTIMIZING A PROGRAM

The suggestions in this chapter have been written with the idea that they would be read and followed when writing the program. But often a particular production program is to be optimized because it runs too long.

Maybe when the program was originally written no one thought it would be used much, so no care was taken to make it efficient. Or possibly the program has been modified extensively and has become inefficient. Now the program is used quite often and it consumes too much time, or possibly it is close to exceeding available storage. The result is that an effort is to be made to make it more efficient.

Before explaining a method to optimize a program I will return to the subject of algorithm selection. If a program must be optimized, the algorithm used in the program should be carefully examined. The basic method chosen for the problem has a major effect on the speed and core usage of the program.

Maybe a different algorithm should have been chosen and optimizing the old algorithm will not provide the gain desired. The following assumes that the original algorithm is a sound and reasonable one, but a programmer who needs to optimize his program should never make that assumption.

Segment the Program

When optimizing an already written program, the first step is to divide the program into segments or subprograms. Attempt to find autonomous units that do a logical task. Some programs are difficult to segment this way, but such segmentation will pay dividends in many ways. Subprograms with 40 or 50 statements are ideal. If you use smaller ones, there will be too many; if larger, they probably will not be logical units. Most large programs should already be segmented into subprograms. If the program is already divided into subprograms, then this task is much easier. Once the subprograms are established there are three things you need to estimate:

1. What percentage of total time does each subprogram use?
2. What percentage of optimization is possible in each subprogram?
3. How many man hours are necessary to achieve this goal?

The next three subsections will discuss each question in detail.

Time the Subprograms

Once the program is divided into subprograms, each subprogram should be timed to determine what percentage of time is used in each subprogram. It is important to actually time each subprogram in order to establish which sections are the most time consuming.

If estimates or guesses are used to allocate time to each subprogram, mistakes will often take place and the optimization will fail.

A superficial analysis will lead to the wrong subprogram being chosen for optimization. Once the actual time is established, the subprograms that use the most time should receive the greatest effort toward optimization. For example, maybe the program is divided into four subprograms and the timing is:

Subprogram A   5%
Subprogram B   60%
Subprogram C   15%
Subprogram D   20%

From this table we can see that even if subprogram A was eliminated (which usually is not possible or desirable), we would save only 5% of the total program time. Thus, the major optimization effort will probably be put into subprogram B. This is where the greatest saving is possible.

If it is not possible to get actual timings of the subprograms, another approach is to count the number of statements, preferably from an assembly listing of a higher level language. Loops should be treated multiplicatively. This will give a fairly good indication of the percentage of time for each subunit, but actual timing is much better.

Most programs have one *critical point* that is responsible for using the majority of the execution time. It is not unusual to have a single small section of code responsible for better than 50% of all execution time. This section is obviously the first section to attempt to optimize.

After the first critical point is optimized it is a good idea to re-analyze the program again. For now there may be a different critical point that also can be optimized. This process can be repeated as many times as significant results are obtained.

Execution-Time Profiles

In the past, actually timing segments of a program was the best possible method available for examining the program for time-consuming waste. Now, execution-time profiles are becoming available. Appendix II contains an excellent paper on FETE, which analyzes a FORTRAN program while it is being executed and actually lists the number of times each command is executed and the cost involved. Execution profiles are also available in COBOL, PL/I, and ALGOL W.

Even programmers not working in FORTRAN will be interested in the results disclosed in this paper. For example, they have discovered by using FETE to analyze programs that often 3% of the code constitutes 50% of the execution time. Thus, if a programmer wishes to optimize his program and has FETE to tell him which commands to optimize, good improvement can be made with minimum effort.

One side advantage of using execution profiles comes during testing and debugging. Since execution profiles give frequency counts, they can be used to discover statements that have not been tested. A statement executed with zero frequency has not been tested. Likewise, statement frequency counts can be used to see if a particular statement was executed the exact number of times expected.

Estimate Possible Improvement

Once an accurate estimation of percentage total time is established an estimation of possible improvement should be made. If a subprogram accounts for a large percentage of total time, but little improvement is possible, then the resulting effort would be fruitless.

When estimating possible improvement only the approximate magnitude of improvement is necessary or possible. It is not important whether the possible improvement is 20% or 25%. What is important is whether it would be 5% or 70%.

Determining the possible improvement is not a trivial task. Experience will probably be the best guide. This chapter has suggested many techniques for writing an efficient program. Thus one can look for statements that can be modified by using the suggestions given in this chapter. Careful examination of loops and input/output are always the most rewarding.

We can now establish a product which will indicate the possible improvement. If we have a subprogram that uses 50% of the total program time, but offers only a 5% increase in efficiency, we would end up with a 2.5% (.50 * .05 = .025) total increase in efficiency. A different subprogram that uses 10% of total program time, but offers a 50% increase in efficiency, would result in a 5% (.50 * 10 = .05) total increase in efficiency. Thus the second subprogram should be chosen first for optimization since the final result is largest. It is important that the product of % usage and % improvement be

considered in order not to spend a great deal of time and effort optimizing the wrong subprogram.

Necessary Effort

Along with determining the possible improvement, we should
estimate the amount of work necessary to accomplish this improvement. Now, we can calculate a weighted sum for each subprogram
as follows:

$$\frac{\% \text{ time } * \% \text{ improvement}}{\text{effort needed}}$$

The subprogram with the highest weighted sum would usually be the
first one selected for optimization.

The major advantage of careful selection of the subprogram to be
optimized is that valuable resources (programmer and computer time)
can be assigned where they will do the most good. If resources are
assigned unwisely, a great deal of effort can result in little increase in
efficiency. If there is not enough time or justification to redo the
complete program, the most fruitful subprograms can be worked on.

There are two approaches to optimizing an already existing program: clean up and redesign. Both have advantages and disadvantages.
The clean-up approach consists of correcting obvious sloppiness in
the original program. In addition, any language peculiarities that lend
themselves to optimization can be exploited. Many of the suggestions in this chapter will help improve the efficiency. The positive
side of this approach is that it doesn't take much time. The negative
side is that, by simply cleaning up the original program, the gain in
efficiency is usually not spectacular.

The second approach is redesign of the original program. If the
program is divided into subprograms, redesign can be done on the
subprogram that is most time consuming. While redesign usually gets
best results, it is also the most costly.

Hopefully, a great deal has been learned from the first effort to
write a program and this information can be used during redesigning.
Redesign is especially helpful if the program has been changed extensively. Often revisions will have changed the goal of the original
program. Possibly the program has been in a constant state of revision for a period of time. Now the program's results seem to be

accepted and revisions will be less extensive and often. Then, using the knowledge gained and the new goals, redesign should bring about perceptible savings in program time.

COMPUTER LORE

Each computer and compiler has some efficiency lore. This is information, if known and used, that will make a program compile or execute more efficiently. But information of this type is usually very machine dependent and often is available only from assembly listings.

An example in FORTRAN for one rather popular computer is that if statement numbers are evenly distributed over their range, the program will compile faster. This is because, for its internal use, the compiler places statement numbers in tables and these tables are divided into strings that are searched many times during compilation. If the number of entries in each string is approximately equal, the average time required to find a statement number is reduced.

Statement numbers are assigned to five strings in the statement number table according to the last digit in the statement number. Statement numbers ending in 0 or 1 are placed in the first string; those ending in 2 or 3 are placed in the second; those ending in 4 or 5 are placed in the third; etc. Thus, statement numbers that are evenly distributed will decrease compilation time.

A similar situation occurs with variable names. Names are assigned to a string according to the length of the variable name. Names that are one character long are assigned to the first string, names two characters long are assigned to the second string; etc. Thus, if names are fairly evenly distributed over the different strings, less search time will be needed to find each name.

These comments on computer lore are only to illustrate that, if efficiency is very important, you must not only know the general rules in this chapter but also learn some of the lore of your computer and its compiler and operating system.

CONCLUSION

It seems evident that the writing of efficient programs will continue to be important for the foreseeable future. The writing of efficient programs has assumed a renewed importance with the availability of the mini-computers. The development of storage efficient programming can mean the difference between being able to run a program in a straight-forward manner, or having to segment the program for an overlay, resorting to assembly language, looking for a larger computer, or not solving the problem. Programs that do not use computer time efficiently can rapidly absorb all computer time, thus reducing the number of problems that can be solved.

Programs written in high-level languages are often written only once, then patched, repaired, added to, and thus inflated to the point that available storage is not enough. In the past, if a program would not reside in core because of its size, the solution was always to get larger equipment. But it has been observed that no matter how much core is available, there is never enough. Instead, a few techniques, such as discussed in this chapter, once learned can continue to pay dividends in faster and smaller programs. Otherwise, a computer installation will find itself continually plagued by programs too slow or too large.

EXERCISES

1. Is there an optimizing compiler available for your programming language? If so, what type of optimizations are made?

2. What compiler options are used at your installation to speed compilation during debugging?

3. What compiler options are used at your installation to speed program execution?

4. On your compiler, are there compiling options to minimize storage usage in object programs at the expense of execution speed? Is it possible to maximize execution speed at the expense of storage?

5. Select two different commands in your programming language and develop timing tests to see which command executes faster.

6. What are the definitions of:
   (a) program overlay?
   (b) folding?

    (c) reducing the strength of an operation?

    (d) eliminating redundant expressions?

    (e) collapsing a loop?

    (f) removing invariant expressions?

    (g) unrolling a loop?

7. Obtain an assembly listing of one of your high-level language programs. Examine the assembly listing to see which program statements generate the most code.

8. How should nested loops be arranged to reduce loop initializations and testings?

9. What areas of a program are usually the most productive for optimization?

10. What is the most important factor for writing an efficient program?

11. Describe an efficient algorithm for finding all the factors of a number. For example, the factors of 12 are 1, 2, 3, 4, 6, 12. If you are not positive it is the most efficient algorithm, program it.

12. *Chess Players.* Describe an algorithm for placing the maximum number of knights on a chess board so no knight can capture another.

13. In your programming language, what things can be done at compilation to speed up execution?

14. What type of programs should be optimized? What type should not?

15. What is the most efficient type of variables in your programming language for subscripts?

16. What is the most efficient type of variables in your programming language for numerous noninteger calculations?

17. How does your compiler handle the following expression?

$$B = 3.0 \ / \ 4.0 \ * \ B$$

Is the constant expression calculated at compile time or execution time? A look at the assembly code will usually tell you the answer.

18. Why is an optimizing compiler still necessary even if the programmer does optimizations?

19. Does your compiler store constants in the correct form so conversions are unnecessary during execution?

20. When is it less efficient to use a loop than to use straight-line coding?

21. How do you do a program overlay in your programming language?

22. Is there an equivalence method in your programming language? How would you set up two arrays so they use the same storage locations?

23. In your programming language, how can you initialize variables (arrays) at compile time instead of at execution time?

24. Put the following arithmetic operations in order of fastest to slowest:
    (a) Division
    (b) Square Root
    (c) Addition
    (d) Exponentiation
    (e) Multiplication
    (f) Subtraction

25. Code the following in the most efficient manner:
    (a) $B = \dfrac{4A}{3}$
    (b) `C = P**0.5`
    (c) $Y = 5x^4 + 3x^2 - 2x + 2$
    (d) `T = COS(THETA) - COS(THETA)**2.0`
    (e) `PUT = COST/2 * 4 * K`
    (f) `T = P/2 + (6 - R)/4 - T/2`
    (g) `Y = 6 + T**5.0`
    (h) `T = 2 * PI/4`
    (i) `IF A < B  OR  C > D  THEN  X=4`
       `                    ELSE  Y=0;`

26. On your computer, how long does each of the following operations take? (Look up the machine instructions.)
    (a) Integer addition
    (b) Real addition

(c) Integer multiplication

(d) Real multiplication

(e) Real division

27. Obtain an assembly language listing of a high-level language program. See if you can determine which statements seem to be inefficient.

28. Does your computer use double buffers for input/output? Can you request more or fewer buffers? If yes, try changing the number of buffers and see if it will change the time used by a program.

29. Find a program that needs optimizing and try to optimize it by using the techniques discussed in this chapter.

30. Can you think of techniques for optimizing your program that are not discussed in this chapter? If so, send me a list of your new techniques.

31. Write a program to read a positive integer N and then sum all the integers from 1 to N.

32. *Compound Interest.* Assume $100.00 is to be deposited for 55 years at 6% compounded quarterly. Program this problem.

33. Assume I, J, K, and L are positive integers less than 20. Write a program to find the values which satisfy the equation:

$$I^3 + J^3 + K^3 = L^3$$

Your program should be both readable and efficient. Compare your solution to someone else's solution.

34. Sort problems are good tests of algorithm selection and efficiency techniques. Read N numbers, then sort the numbers in ascending sequence and print the sorted numbers. If you have a function that generates random numbers, use it to generate 1,000 random numbers and sort these numbers. Compare your program to another program to see which program is the fastest.

35. *Table Searching.* Generate a table of 1,000 random integers between 1 and 10,000. Write a program that reads a positive integer less than 10,000 and then determines if the number is in

the table. You can organize the table and searching any way you want to do it.

36. *Diagonal Matrix.* A diagonal matrix has zeros everywhere except in the principal diagonal. Write a program to multiply two diagonal matrices.

37. *Symmetric Matrix.* A symmetric matrix is identical with its transpose. That is, for any element $a_{ij} = a_{ji}$. Write a program to multiply two symmetric matrices. Is your program efficient?

38. *Triangular Matrix.* A lower-triangular matrix has all zeros above the principal diagonal. Write an efficient program to add two large lower-triangular matrices.

39. *Repeated Elements.* Assume you have a large rectangular matrix. Some of the columns in the matrix are identical. Devise a method for storing the matrix without storing any identical columns more than once. Now assume you have two matrices identical in size and add the matrices. Do not assume that the two matrices have identical columns.

40. *Sparse Matrices.* Assume that you have two very large matrices (that is, 1,000 by 1,000 elements each) and most of the elements (95%) are zero. Devise a technique to store the arrays efficiently. Then write a program to add arrays and multiply arrays.

41. Simulations usually require efficient programming if the problem is to be solved in a reasonable amount of time. Both problems 35 and 36 in Chapter VI require efficient programming techniques.

42. Wolf Island is a 20 by 20 plot populated by rabbits, male wolves, and female wolves, all acting wild. In the beginning, a few of each kind of the inhabitants are scattered about the island. Rabbits are rather stupid; at each time step they move with equal probability to one of the eight squares in their neighborhood (excepting as restricted by the coastline). 1/9 of the time they therefore simply sit still. Each rabbit also has a probability of 0.2 of becoming two rabbits. Each female wolf also moves randomly unless there is a rabbit on one of the eight neighboring squares, in which case she gives chase. If she and

the rabbit end up on the same square, she eats it and gains one "fat." Otherwise, she loses 0.1 "fat." Zero-fat wolves are dead. Each male wolf behaves like the females unless there are no rabbits nearby but there is a female on one of the eight neighboring squares, in which case he gives chase. If a male and female end up on the same square with no rabbits to eat, they produce an offspring with a random sex.

Program the ecological simulation suggested and watch the population counts over several time periods. (Thanks to Bill McKeeman for this problem.)

43. The previous simulation is inherently unstable (Wolf Island is destined to be a desert). Add a hedgerow (an area forbidden to wolves) and observe the results.

44. On the following problems you must program an efficient algorithm and decide how much effort to put into the problem. The solution may be very difficult or even impossible.

a) Find two integers m, n such that $m^2 = 2n^2$.

b) Find some integer solutions for x, y, z where $x^3 + y^3 + z^3 = 1$.

$$\text{Two solutions are} \qquad \begin{array}{ll} x = y = 1 & z = -1 \\ x = y = -4 & z = 5 \end{array}$$

c) Find all solutions of the equation $x^3 - y^2 = 18$ where x, y are integers.

d) For n, x, y, z integers and $n > 2$, is there a solution for $x^n + y^n = z^n$?

e) Generate a map so that more than four colors are needed to color the map in order that no two contiguous districts shall be of the same color.

f) Write a program to generate some interesting mazes with only one path.

REFERENCES

Abrahams, Paul. "Compiler Pessimization." *Datamation*. April 1, 1971.

Allen, F. E. "Program Optimization." *Annual Review in Automatic Programming*, Vol. 5. New York: Pergamon Press. 1969.

Chapin, Ned. *Programming Computers for Business Applications.* New York: McGraw-Hill Book Company, Inc. 1961.

Cohn, Charles Erwin. "Efficient Programming in FORTRAN." *Software Age.* June, 1968.

Constantine, Larry L. "A Modular Approach to Program Optimization." *Computers and Automation.* March, 1967.

Constantine, Larry L. *Concepts in Program Design.* Somerville, Mass.: Paragon Press. 1969.

Denning, Peter J. "Virtual Memory." *Computing Surveys.* September, 1970.

Gries, David. *Compiler Construction for Digital Computers,* 1971. New York: John Wiley & Sons, Inc.

Ignalls, Daniel H. H. "FETE: A FORTRAN Execution Time Estimator." Dept. of Computer Science, Stanford University. February

1971. 11 pages. Available from National Technical Information Service. U.S. Department of Commerce, Springfield, Va. 22151. Document number PB-198 510. $3.00.

Knuth, Donald E. "An Empirical Study of FORTRAN Programs." Computer Science Dept., Stanford University. 1970. 42 pages. Available from Clearinghouse for Federal Scientific & Technical Information, Springfield, Va. 22151. $3.00.

Larson, Chris. "The Efficient Use of FORTRAN." *Datamation.* August 1, 1971.

"Minimizing Memory Requirements for COBOL Programs." *B2500 and B3500 Technical Newsletter.* 1042272-006. 5-71. 18 pages. Burroughs Corporation.

"Optimization and Efficient Performances." *IBM System/360 Operating System PL/I (F) Language Reference Manual.* IBM Corporation.

"Programming Considerations." *IBM System/360 Operating System Basic FORTRAN IV (E) Programmer's Guide.* IBM Corporation. C28-6603.

"Programming Techniques." *IBM System/360 Operating System, USA Standard COBOL Programmer's Guide.* IBM Corporation.

Rohl, J. M. "FORTRAN Programming Considerations." Technical Report No. 27, April, 1969. Computer Centre, The Australian National University Canberra, A.C.T.

Rustin, Randall, editor. *Design and Optimization of Compilers*, 1972. Englewood Cliffs, N.J.: Prentice-Hall, Inc.

"Suggestions for the Efficient Use of the B2500/B3500 COBOL Compiler." Prepared by Programming Systems Department, Burroughs Corporation, Systems M & E Group, Medium Systems Plant. Pasadena, Calif.

Walker, Ewing S. "Optimization of Tape Operations." *Software Age.* August/September, 1970.

Walter, Arline Bohl, and Marilyn Bohl. "From Better to Best Tips for Good Programming." *Software Age.* November, 1969.

Walter, Kenneth G. "Compiler Optimization of Object Programs." A Thesis submitted to Case Institute of Technology. Cleveland, Ohio. 1966.

Weinberg, Gerald M. *PL/I Programming*, 1970. New York: McGraw-Hill Book Company, Inc.

"1130 FORTRAN Programming Techniques." C20-1642. IBM Corporation.

One difficulty with obscure bugs is that the probability
of their appearance increases with time and wider use.
A bug-free program is an abstract theoretical concept.

Bloody instructions which, being learned,
return to plague the inventor.   Macbeth.

IV

Program Debugging

Few occupations offer greater opportunities for making errors than programming. These errors are called *bugs*; and the art of locating these bugs is called debugging. One measure of a programmer's proficiency is his ability to find and correct his own bugs. While beginning programmers cannot locate and correct their bugs, experienced programmers can. All programmers have program bugs.

Programmers are often trained in programming, but seldom are they trained in debugging. Since debugging a program takes longer and is much more difficult than writing the original program, it is unfortunate that more time is not spent in showing how to debug. Estimates of the amount of time spent debugging verge from 50% to 90%. Writing a program is like writing a report. Both require a first draft (before bugs) and a final draft (after bugs). Seldom is the first draft the final draft in writing or programming.

There is very little information available on how to debug a program. Debugging is commonly called an art to avoid the difficult task of teaching debugging. Debugging is very dependent on the environment; that is, the machine, the language, the operating system, the problem, and even the individual program.

It is certainly true that each language, compiler, and machine lends itself to certain types of bugs or errors. The simplest example of this is syntax errors that are very language dependent. Very little information is available on the relationship between a language and the number and difficulty of bugs.

This chapter will cover the subject of source-language debugging. For those who like to read dumps and do arithmetic in hexadecimal or octal I offer my warmest encouragement. But one of the major reasons for using source language is to be able to avoid learning machine language. Machine-language debugging has the disadvantage that it is machine dependent. Thus, changes of computer due to new models or a new job can make all machine-language information useless. It is my belief that skills learned should be as resistant to technological changes as possible. That is why it is more valuable to learn how to debug programs in source languages than in machine languages. Machine-language and memory-dump debugging is usually a desirable tool only as a last resort after all other methods have failed.

The advantages of source-language debugging are:

1. It is not necessary to know machine language.
2. Output can be printed in readable form along with identifying labels.
3. Techniques from the source language can be used to debug the program.

DEBUGGING versus TESTING

Many programmers confuse the debugging and testing stage of checking out programs. If a program is obviously not working correctly, then it is being debugged. Thus debugging always starts with some evidence of program failure. If the program seems to be working correctly, then it is being tested. Often after tests have been run the program will fall back to the debugging stage. Testing determines that an error exists; debugging localizes the cause of the error. Thus, there is overlapping of the two stages. Programming time should be allotted for both stages in order to emphasize that both stages need to be done.

Beginning programmers often feel only the program needs to be debugged. That is, once the program works for one carefully selected group of data, they believe it will work for all other data. They are then surprised when, after using and believing the results for several runs, the program produces obviously incorrect output. Then all previous output is of questionable veracity.

Usually, there are two approaches to debugging: either a great deal of programmer time is spent trying to avoid and detect bugs manually, or the machine is used to do most of the detecting of bugs. The choice of the alternatives is governed by the amount of machine time available. There is a natural tendency (due to human laziness) to try to push most of the debugging work off on the machine. If machine time is available, this is all right since the machine is better equipped to finding bugs anyway.

There is, however, another approach to debugging. In this approach debugging overlaps with the writing stage of programming. Some programmers prefer to write a few lines of code and then attempt to execute those additional lines of code to see if they work properly. Programmers who program this way are writing, debugging, and testing as they program. It would be interesting to determine which method of programming is most productive.

This piece-meal approach allows you to ferret out errors as you code. The advantage is that the code is still fresh in your mind, so errors are easier to spot. This approach is similar to dividing your program into subroutines.

DEBUGGING IS THE NEXT HURDLE

Debugging is probably the next hurdle to be crossed in computing. Until the late 1950s hardware was the limiting factor in computing. Everyone was trying to squeeze their program into 4K of memory and have everything ready when the next read was available. The second epoch was software. Now, with ALGOL, FORTRAN, COBOL, PL/I, et al., sufficient software is available.

The present bottleneck is debugging. We now have machines big and fast enough to execute most useful programs, and software varied enough to get those programs written.

Some people have assumed that, as computer languages and compilers become more sophisticated, bugs will disappear. A few characteristics are ignored with this assumption. Logic errors cannot be discovered by compilers because that assumes the compiler knows what you want to do. If the compiler knew what you wanted to do, it could also write the program.

Programs have increased in size and complexity, thus keeping about a constant level of bugs.

The First Bug

There is a story about the first program bug that goes as follows:

Early in the history of computers when the Whirlwind I at M.I.T. was first switched on, it failed to run. A frantic check of the wiring and hardware failed to indicate anything wrong. Finally, in desperation it was decided to check the program, then a small strip of paper tape. Thus the error was discovered: the programmers' Pandora's box, a plague of bugs descends on future generations of programmers.

ERRORS IN PROBLEM DEFINITION

A common situation is that once the program is written the user finds out that the results are not the desired results. This can be because the programmer and the user did not understand each other, or because the user did not really know what he wanted. If the incorrect program does help the user discover what he wants, or shows the programmer what the user really wanted, then all is not for nothing.

Sometimes only when incorrect results are generated can the original problem be carefully redefined. Bad program definition results in a program correctly solving the wrong problem. Usually, the entire program must be reprogrammed. Insist on a new time schedule when the program must be redone. Don't allow the incorrect program to use all the resources (programming time, machine time, etc.). A new program is to be written and thus a new schedule is required.

When writing a program for someone else, a warning sign that the program may not be the desired program is the feeling that the problem is not clear. In order to avoid an "incorrect" program, it is best to write down a description of what the program should do, along with a sample. The writing of a description of the desired program forces the person wanting the program to organize his thoughts enough to describe the desired program. Oral instructions on program specifications are notoriously undependable and often lead to violent misunderstandings.

INCORRECT ALGORITHM

Once the problem is correctly defined, the programmer searches for an algorithm or method that will solve the problem. Unfortunately, the programmer may choose an incorrect algorithm or a poor algorithm, in which case he will have to repeat the whole process.

An example of an incorrect algorithm is an iterative method for solving an equation that diverges when another method would correctly calculate the answer. An example of a poor or badly chosen algorithm is an algorithm that correctly calculates the answer, but does it very slowly. Unfortunately, often it is not possible to know a bad algorithm was picked until after it has been tried. But some time and thought should be put into algorithm selection in order not to have to redo every program. There are quite a few books available on programming techniques and some of these have programming algorithms in them. Readers who wish to avoid incorrect algorithms should familiarize themselves with books within their own fields.

ERRORS IN ANALYSIS

Errors in analysis consist of either overlooking possibilities or incorrectly solving the problem. The overlooking of possibilities includes things like not considering negative values or small or large numbers.

Incorrectly solving the problem is usually a major or minor logic error. Here are some possibilities:

1. Not initializing variables.
2. Incorrect termination of a loop.
3. Incorrect indexing of a loop.
4. Omitted loop initialization.
5. Interchanging of two or more paths after leaving a decision statement.

The best way to debug is to minimize the need for it. A good functional design followed by a fairly detailed flowchart or synopsis will result in better coding.

Flowcharts will help prevent many errors. Flowcharts can also be used for reference while debugging to see if any errors did occur. A technique to check a flowchart for correctness is to take the problem definition a second time a few days later and redraw the flowchart. Then the first and second flowcharts can be compared to see where they differ. This may seem a waste of time, but errors at this level may be catastrophic later on and require major program revision.

GENERAL ERRORS

After an appropriate algorithm has been selected for solving a particular problem, there are five possible errors that can occur during programming, regardless of the programming language used. They are:

1. Lack of knowledge or misunderstanding about the language or machine can cause errors. An example is the programmer using a command or function that performs differently than expected. This can be the result of a systems change of which the programmer is unaware.
2. A general error is error in programming the algorithm. Perhaps the program instructions are inconsistent with the series of events required by the algorithm; examples are logic errors or coding errors, such as putting a minus sign where a plus sign is needed.
3. Syntax errors also occur.
4. Syntactically correct statements may cause execution errors; examples are division by zero or negative square roots.
5. A fifth general error is a data error caused by anomalous data. A mathematical operation performed on an alphabetic piece of data is a typical example.

With the exception of syntax errors, all of these general errors are discoverable during testing which results in the program reverting to the debugging stage. Table 4.1 summarizes the errors discussed so far.

Table 4.1 **Common Programming Errors**

1. Error in problem definition	Correctly solving the wrong problem.
2. Incorrect algorithm.	Selecting an algorithm that solves the problem incorrectly or badly.
3. Errors in analysis.	Incorrect programming of the algorithm.
4. Semantic error.	Failure to understand how a command works.
5. Syntax error.	Failure to follow the rules of the programming language.
6. Execution error.	Failure to predict the possible ranges in calculations (i.e., division by zero, etc.)
7. Data error.	Failure to anticipate the ranges of data.

PHYSICAL ERRORS

There are eight physical errors that can cause program bugs. They are:

1. Missing program cards.
2. Interchanging of program cards.
3. Additional program cards (that is, failure to remove corrected cards).
4. Missing data.
5. Data out of order.
6. Incorrect data format.
7. Missing job control (monitor) cards.
8. Referring to the wrong program listing.

Careful handling of card decks can help prevent these errors. If the missing or out-of-sequence program cards do not generate syntax errors, they can be very difficult to locate.

Programs should always be consecutively numbered. This helps to prevent or discover most of the physical errors involving program decks. Program decks that are sequence numbered also facilitate the locating of cards during debugging.

Data should be carefully edit-checked and echo-printed to avoid data errors. Echo-printing means printing all data that is read.

PROGRAM DECK MARKING

All program decks should be marked with a wide ink marker (Magic Marker, etc.). Each subroutine should have separate markings as follows:

1. Mark first card on the face with FC.
2. Mark last card on the back LC.
3. Mark program name on the tops of the deck.
4. Mark diagonal or cross strips on the top of the deck.

This makes identification and location easy during debugging. It will also help indicate shuffled decks.

SIMPLE CODING

Simple straightforward coding is a great help when debugging. It is easier to avoid and detect errors if the program is written in an orderly and logical manner. In the early stages of writing a complicated program one should not hesitate to rewrite sections if it will simplify the program. Programming tricks should be completely avoided. The more "tricks" used when programming, the more difficult it is for you to debug your own program. And tricky programs are impossible to debug by someone who did not write the original program.

My final mention of simple coding will only refer you back to Chapter I on programming style. Many of the suggestions of program style can make your program more readable, and thus easier to debug.

CORRECTNESS

Programs are logically correct only in a relative sense. It is relative to a certain class of data. A program to find the largest common divisor of two input numbers is correct only if the two numbers are integers. If input is either zero or fractional, then the program would not operate correctly. Thus, the domain of data over which the program will operate correctly must be carefully defined. Program statements are needed to verify that the input data stay within the necessary domain of definition.

In order for a program to be acceptable it must be correct. There are two ways in which a program can be incorrect:

1. The syntax is incorrect.
2. The program provides incorrect answers.

Syntax correctness means that variable names must be correctly formed, arithmetic and logical operations must follow the syntax rules, etc.

SYNTAX ERRORS

The compiler's discovery of syntax errors is the most important and taken for granted stage of debugging. The greater the number of errors discovered and corrected at this stage, the easier all later debugging and testing will be. The beginning programmer assumes that all syntax errors are discovered at this stage. The more experienced and cynical programmer knows that many subtle "syntax" errors will not be discovered by the compiler. The trend has been to provide more of these diagnostics and to make them more specific about the error they are reporting.

If a syntax error is defined as "anything that violates the language specifications," then many syntax errors are not discovered. An uninitialized variable, a branch into the middle of a DO loop, and an out-of-range subscript are just a few of the errors commonly missed. Results in these operations are undefined. If statements like the above are compiled, they will cause the program to act in mysterious ways that can be quite difficult to detect.

The reason detecting syntax errors is so important is that these errors are sure to cause trouble in the execution. Moreover, the compiler requires the syntax errors to be corrected before attempting execution so the errors are certain to be corrected.

Examples of syntax errors are:

1. Required punctuation missing.
2. Unmatched parentheses.
3. Missing parentheses.

4. Incorrectly formed statements.
5. Incorrect variable names.
6. Arithmetic operators used incorrectly.
7. Misspelling of reserved words.

Another variety of syntax errors involves the interaction of two or more statements. Some examples are:

1. Conflicting instructions.
2. Nontermination of loops.
3. Duplicate or missing labels.
4. Not declaring arrays.
5. Illegal transfer.

If a compiler does not carefully analyze the interaction of two or more commands, it often misses some of the above errors. For example, some compilers will not warn the programmer that he is transferring illegally into a DO loop.

Other errors that are often discovered by the compiler when checking syntax are:

1. Undeclared or incorrectly declared variables.
2. Keypunch errors.
3. Use of illegal characters.

Most syntax errors are very language and machine dependent, so there is not much that can be said in detail about correcting individual syntax errors. But there are a few general hints that can be given on syntax errors.

One hint for correcting syntax errors is that when a great many errors are generated, just correct the obvious errors and rerun the program. Some syntax error messages are spurious, that is, caused by other syntax errors, so a great deal of time should not be spent trying to understand a syntax error message if the error is not immediately obvious. Spurious error messages are usually especially prevalent when something serious has been omitted in the program, such as variable or array declare statements.

The second observation is don't be afraid to read the program language manual. When trying to correct nonobvious syntax errors, a reading of syntax rules for the particular command will usually indicate the error.

At last resort, start looking for someone a little more experienced to help you. But remember, if you bother your helper too much, he will probably get tired of "doing your programming." Ask for help only after you have tried and failed. Programmers are usually naturally interested in unusual errors, but bored with trivial errors that you should be able to figure out for yourself.

THE COMPILER

The compiler used greatly affects the amount of debugging needed. A good debugging compiler can often reduce debugging time by half. A *debugging compiler* checks for more errors than a regular compiler. Syntax is more carefully examined and the interaction of commands is checked. More importantly, numerous checks are done during execution of the source program. Uninitialized variables, out-of-range subscripts, and illegal transfers are flagged during execution. But all this additional checking requires extra time, so execution time is usually much slower.

FORTRAN users have long had the benefit of the debugging compiler WATFIV. Long experience with this compiler has proven that debugging time can be significantly reduced with a good compiler. In addition, bugs are removed early in program construction.

But these compilers must be purchased and do not come supplied with the computer. My opinion is that it is difficult to spend too much on a good debugging compiler. When you consider that 70% of the programmer's time and a high percentage of machine time are spent debugging, then a good debugging compiler will soon pay for itself.

The University of Waterloo supplies two debugging compilers, COBOL WATBOL and FORTRAN WATFIV. Cornell University has a PL/I compiler called PL/C. Finally, there is ALGOL W from Stanford University. Thus, all the major programming languages have a debugging compiler.

Errors the Compiler Cannot Detect

There are many errors which the compiler cannot detect when the statements used are correctly formed. Examples of undetectable errors are:

1. Omission of part of the program.
2. Branching the wrong way on a decision statement.
3. Using the wrong format for reading data.
4. Incorrect values in loops, such as the initial value, increment, or terminal value.
5. Arrays too small or incorrect array subscripting.
6. Failure to consider all possibilities that may occur in the data or in the calculations.

Here is an example showing why subscripting errors cannot be discovered during compilation. If an array has 10 elements and subscripts are calculated by using variables, then the array bounds may be exceeded. But they are exceeded during execution. For instance, given an array of $A(10)$ and

$$I = 4 * K$$
$$\vdots$$
$$A(I) =$$

Whenever K is greater than 2 the array subscript will be incorrect, but this cannot be discovered at compilation.

Other errors that cannot be discovered during compilation include incorrect mode of arguments in the call statements. That is, a subprogram expects to get an integer argument and is passed a real number. This type of error cannot be discovered at compilation, because each subprogram can be compiled separately. Thus, the compiler cannot check to see if the mode of the arguments of the subprogram is compatible with the mode of the arguments in the calling program. This type of error can be caught during execution if information about type of variables is supplied by the compiler, or it can be caught on a compile and execute by a good debugging compiler.

If an error passes undetected by the compiler, the object program will nevertheless be compiled from the source program. Then the object program will cause an abnormal end at some point during execution. If no abnormal end occurs, one will simply obtain an output that is incorrect, and no indication will be given that the output is incorrect. Testing of the program is used to discover any errors that the compiler did not locate.

Other errors which can be caught by the compiler (but seldom are) are:

1. Unused labels.
2. Undefined variables.
3. Variables that are declared but never used.
4. Checking function arguments for correct type.
5. Checking format specifications for correct type.

The above errors can all be discovered at the compilation stage. There are other errors that can be discovered only during execution. Some compilers generate code (such as checking subscript ranges) that will check for certain errors during execution. The more that is checked for, the less work one has to do on removing bugs.

TYPES OF DEBUGGING

Debugging starts after all syntax error messages are eliminated. Use simple test data to start the debugging. If the test data produces correct results, continue testing. If the program does not produce correct results, five situations are possible:

1. The program did not compile, but there are no syntax errors.
2. The program compiles, executes, but produces no output.
3. The program compiles, executes, but terminates prematurely.
4. The program compiles, executes, but produces incorrect output.
5. The program does not stop running (or infinite loop).

Case 1: Compilation Not Completed

This situation is rather rare and indicates a catastrophic error someplace in the program. System error messages usually appear in this situation. If so, they can be used to help locate the error. But a great deal of experience is usually needed to interpret these messages, so help may be needed. Part of your debugging skill is often having a friend who will help you.

If no one is available to help you and you can't find the error yourself, the best approach is to try to isolate the error. One does this by breaking the program into smaller executable segments and attempting to compile the smaller segments. Keep segmenting the program until a segment will compile. Then start adding segments until the program stops compiling. The last segment added is the section with the error in it. Either careful inspection of the error section or segmenting of the error section should help indicate the statement preventing compilation. This method is a very undesirable method, so use it only as a last resort. Finding a knowledgeable friend to help you is a much better method.

Case 2: Execution, but No Output

The program executes, but does not produce any output. Some progress has been made, but not much. This type of error can be caused by a logic error or a system error. An example of a logic error of this type is a program that starts execution and then branches to end of job before producing any output. This type of error can be located by using the techniques suggested in the section on locating errors, further on in this chapter.

The system error is caused by some fatal error with which the operating system will not allow execution to continue. The interruption of your program execution can be generated by the computer hardware, operating system, or your compiled program. There is usually a system error code provided. Hopefully, the system provides some indication of what the error is. But system error messages are usually quite cryptic. Also, there is usually no indication of *where* the error is. If some program output is provided, then there is at least a little indication of where the error is, and it is simply a matter of narrowing down the error location either by debugging traces or by debugging output, both of which are covered in a later section.

Examples of errors which can cause system errors:

1. Division by zero.
2. Branching to a data area and attempting execution.
3. Array subscripts incorrect.
4. Numeric underflow or overflow.

Locating the error in examples one and two can sometimes be extremely difficult. One approach is to reprogram the segment, using an alternate method to achieve the same result. This may be the simplest way to overcome the error if the error is not obvious. A similar solution is to make several copies of the malfunctioning section. Next, vary the coding and rerun the program. Repeat this process until the error goes away or it can be isolated.

Case 3: Terminates Prematurely

The program now compiles, starts execution, provides some output, but then terminates before it should. We have now progressed beyond the first two errors and are usually quite relieved to be obtaining some output.

Since some output is being produced, regular debugging techniques can be used. Errors that stop the program execution prematurely and then provide a system error message are *blow ups* or *cratered*. These are errors so severe that execution cannot continue. This type of error can be located by using the techniques suggested in the section on locating errors, further on in this chapter.

Case 4: Incorrect Answers

The program runs but produces incorrect answers. Experienced programmers always consider themselves lucky when this stage is reached. This probably indicates that the program is basically sound and the logic is almost correct. The rest of the chapter will be devoted to helping debug this type of error.

Case 5: An Infinite Loop

This error is usually not very difficult to find. If you cannot spot the loop immediately, simply add print statements before and after suspected loops. Do not put print statements in the loops; otherwise, thousands of lines of output will usually appear. The print statements will provide output which will indicate which loop is entered but never exited.

GENERAL HINTS

Punch the program all in one-color cards, usually manila. Then punch all debug cards in a different color so they can easily be removed, once the debugging is finished. Statements inserted for debugging should be on a card all by themselves, also to facilitate removal. Use columns 73-80 to punch some message such as DEBUG or REMOVE in all debugging cards. Or use a comment or note to indicate that the debugging card is to be removed after debugging. Then the source listing will clearly indicate what cards are to be removed after debugging.

Do not let any one routine become too large—break it into small routines that can be debugged and tested independently. Think about the debugging stage when writing the original program in order not to write a program that is impossible to debug or test. Develop at least a rough flowchart before starting to program. This flowchart will help to organize your thoughts.

During debugging, it is often helpful to have a list of variables and constants used in the program. This list is usually supplied by the compiler. It can be used to indicate keypunch errors since extra variable names will be available from it.

Isolate problems and fix one at a time. If you make several changes and new trouble arises, you usually won't know which change caused the new error. Also you won't learn what corrected the old error. After you get an error corrected, look it over so you will remember the problem and not make the same error again. If the error causes very unusual output you should attempt to remember the type of error so you will know next time what causes that type of error.

Make changes at the source level only. Never patch a program in machine language. Program patches destroy the documentation of a high-level language and are very prone to introducing errors.

Don't blame the computer. Computers and their compilers are quite reliable today. If the computer stops working, it is usually immediately obvious to the machine-room staff. Computers don't make small mistakes, only big ones.

Realize that there will probably be mistakes. Even good programmers make mistakes. But good programmers realize that there will be mistakes, find them, correct them, and get all the bugs out of the program. Amateur programmers take for granted that there are no mistakes, or leave some bugs in which result in either consistent or occasional spurious output. Quite often, by explaining to someone what you are *trying* to accomplish, you will discover the error.

When debugging, it is common to rerun a program many times. Thus care must be taken with output or the many runs will add to the confusion. All output should have the date and the time on it. Throw away unneeded output in order to avoid confusion. But remember that attempts at correcting one error can often introduce new errors. Then you usually wish you could get back to a previous stage where the errors were less serious.

Thus it is usually necessary to save some of the previous outputs. One solution is to take all old program listings away from your desk and stack them one on top of another in a different location. By storing old program listings in a different location you will remove them so you don't confuse them with current runs, but will still have them for reference if needed. Then you can dispose of the old program listings at your leisure.

If you have saved dated output, then it is easy to backup. One should always save the most recent program run or two, because programs can be easily lost, dropped, gotten out of sequence, or otherwise damaged. Then a previous run or deck is worth a lot. If you wish to be very careful, you can occasionally reproduce your source deck. This provides a ready backup if one is ever needed.

After correcting one bug, examine output carefully to make sure other bugs have not been introduced. This is especially true when changing the logic of the program. Modifying the logical structure of a program might correct one error, but will very often introduce new errors.

UNDEFINED VARIABLES

A common source of program errors is undefined or not initialized variables. Every variable that is used in an output statement, or on the right side of an equal sign in an arithmetic statement, or in a logical statement, must have been computed on the left-hand side of an equal sign, used in an input statement, or inputted as subroutine parameter. That is, you can't use variables that have not been defined by input or computing.

Here are some programming statements.

$$A=1$$
$$B=B+A$$

If B has not previously had a value assigned to it, B is an undefined variable. What actually happens in most languages is that the
old bit pattern left over from previous operations at the storage location assigned to B is used for present value of B. Thus, the value of
B is a random number and anything may happen. A good debugging
compiler will locate undefined variables.

A sure indication of undefined variables is to run the same program and data (with *no changes* in the program or data) and get different results on the two runs. Quite often a program will be used
for a long period before it becomes obvious that there are undefined
variables. This may be because the undefined variable has usually
had a zero assigned to it or it was given a value that didn't cause an
obvious error.

There are two ways to get undefined variables:

By not initializing a variable before it is used.
By keypunching error.

The first type of undefined variable has already been discussed.
Programmers must be careful not to use a variable before it is
defined.

The second type of undefined variable results from keypunch
error. After programs are keypunched they should always be verified
and desk checked to eliminate keypunch errors. Careful selection of
variable names will help eliminate keypunch errors. Names such as
the following are dangerous:

K0 is this K0 (zero) or KØ (letter)
K1 is this K1 (one) or KI (letter)

The letter 0 and number zero are most difficult to locate if interchanged in variable names. Other keypunch errors are discussed in
the keypunch section.

STORAGE MAP

Most compilers have an option called a *storage map*. A storage map is a table of names that appear (or are implied) in the source program. One way to use a storage map is to scan the list for unfamilar variable names. The variable names are in alphabetic order, so you might notice there is one variable name VI, but also one Vl which is keypunch error (punched l instead of I). The storage map would help you locate unfamilar names.

The names are usually provided by type (that is, integer, real, character, etc.). Some storage maps provide a separate list of functions, subroutines, arrays, and constants.

A storage map must usually be requested by job control commands. Each compiler has different grouping and style for its storage map. Storage maps are especially useful when modifying someone else's program because they allow you to get a complete list of all variables used in the program.

CROSS-REFERENCE LIST

A *cross-reference* list indicates where each variable is used in a program. In addition, some cross-reference lists will indicate every place a label, function, or subroutine is referenced. This type of information is often very useful when modifying a program.

Some bugs can also be discovered by a cross-reference list. If a variable is declared but never referenced in the program, this might indicate a misspelled variable name. In addition, a label that is never referenced might indicate an error. Cross-reference lists are usually requested by job control language commands.

KEYPUNCH ERRORS

Keypunch errors in source programs can cause bugs that are very difficult to locate. There are several things that can be done to reduce the number of keypunch errors.

1. Standard coding forms should be used for the programming language. The use of regular lined paper contributes to errors due to wrong columns and makes paragraphing difficult.
2. Use a legible writing device, preferably a soft lead pencil. Soft lead pencils provide readable code and are easy to erase.
3. Code in block letters—not script.
4. Insist that all programs be mechanically verified after key-punching.

There are certain types of keypunch errors that continually cause programmers a great amount of trouble. The following characters are often mis-keypunched:

1 number
I letter
| or
/ Slash
' quotation mark
_____
¬ not
7 seven
> greater than
_____
L letter
< less than
_____
Ø letter (strokes in opposite direction)
Q letter
0 zero
_____
S letter (tails on the letter)
5 five

Ƶ letter
7 seven
2 two
_____
U Make the u round on the bottom plus a tail
V
_____
4 four (close the top of the four)
+ plus
_____
D put tails on the letter D
O letter
_____
G letter
C letter
6 close the number
_____
— break character
‾ minus

Careful attention should be paid to the above characters so that symbols are not interchanged.

DESK CHECKING

As soon as the program is keypunched and verified, the cards should be listed. At many installations this is done automatically as part of the keypunch routine for source decks. This allows the programmer to desk check for keypunch errors or missing cards. Even a casual desk check of the source cards will usually eliminate some errors and thus reduce compiling and debugging time.

It is best to do desk checking right after the keypunching because the program is fresh in your mind. A desk check a week later, after becoming hopelessly involved in debugging, means the original program is no longer fresh enough in your mind to notice a missing or a mispunched card. A few minutes of desk checking can save endless hours of debugging.

There is a tendency to take the attitude that the compiler will catch all keypunch errors. The compiler will catch only keypunch errors that cause syntax errors.

After the program is compared to the keypunch sheets, it should be compared to the flowchart. A command-by-command inspection, while using the flowchart, should eliminate some early bugs. Sometimes it is useful to have a friend (does anyone have such a friend?) compare your program to the flowchart. If small subroutines are used, this job does not seem so arduous; instead of checking one large program, individual tasks can be checked.

Two kinds of error usually indicate undefined variables: UNDERFLOW and OVERFLOW. These words mean numbers that are either too big or too small. Today's computers allow for such a wide range of numbers that almost any calculation can be handled without an underflow or overflow. Unless you know you are using very small or very large numbers, an overflow or underflow error usually indicates an undefined variable some place in the program.

One of the best ways to avoid undefined variables is to initialize as many variables as possible when declaring them. This avoids an error caused by omitting the initialization, improves documentation by exhibiting the initial values in one location, eliminates assignment statements, and thus increases execution efficiency. (This type of initialization is usually done at compile time instead of during execution).

ATTRIBUTES

It is good policy to declare all attributes even if there is a default. The explicit declarations help to document the program. If you do not declare attributes of the variables, the defaults could change, thus causing significant effect on execution of production programs.

Explicit declares of all attributes also have the advantage of making the programmer cognizant of what the attributes are. It is especially important to declare all user-supplied functions and parameter lists to make sure they have the desired attributes. Explicit declares of all variables will eliminate one type of common program bug.

INPUT/OUTPUT ERRORS

One of the first steps in debugging should be the printing of all input. A great many program errors are caused by incorrect reading of input. If input is read incorrectly, a large amount of time can be lost looking for a program bug when the whole problem is due to bad data.

Bad data can be caused by keypunch errors, misunderstandings, or incorrectly specified input formats. By printing input, the programmer can scan the printout and see if input is being read correctly. Inspection of the data cards will help locate only keypunch errors, but will not help discover input format errors. I almost always print my input, since through experience I have learned that printing the input is the only way I can be sure input is read correctly.

Input should be printed immediately after it is read. The immediate outputting of all input is called *echo-checking*. If you delay the echo-checking until later in the program, it is possible the program will never get that far, or it is possible that the storage locations used for input numbers might be altered during execution of the program.

In addition, output should be labeled so it is easy to determine what values belong to which variables. FORTRAN has a NAMELIST command and PL/I has a PUT DATA command that do this easily for you. The DISPLAY or EXHIBIT command in COBOL can be used for easily printing debugging values.

If you are using modules or subprograms, then your input is the parameter values of the module. These should be printed because if they are being received incorrectly, all debugging activity will fail until this is discovered.

Output errors can make a programmer think he has a program bug when the error is just incorrectly specified formats. The most common error is too small output fields or completely incorrect output fields. These errors are usually obvious if the programmer has seen them before. A little bit of experimenting, using too small or incorrect output specification, will illustrate what this type of error looks like.

The other type of output error is not enough decimal places specified on the right of the decimal. For example, when calculating fifths (1/5, 2/5, 3/5 ...), the calculation does not usually calculate exactly on binary computers. So the results are:

$$1/5 = .199...$$
$$2/5 = .399...$$
$$3/5 = .599...$$
$$4/5 = .799...$$

If the output is specified to print only 1 place to the right of the decimal, it would appear as follows on some computers:

$$1/5 = .1$$
$$2/5 = .3$$
$$3/5 = .5$$
$$4/5 = .7$$

This looks like an error since the 9's are not printed. By printing at least 2 places to the right of the decimal it becomes obvious that the output is correct:

$$.19$$
$$.39$$
$$.59$$
$$.79$$

A great amount of time could be wasted trying to figure why the above numbers are incorrect when the real problem is too small output formats. Most systems round output which would eliminate this error.

NUMERICAL PATHOLOGY

If calculations are done by using a desk calculator, the observant operator can notice any major arithmetic faults. But when using a computer, most faults are hidden from view. In addition, calculations are done at a million calculations a second, so it is impossible to trace all calculations. A few of the errors are sufficiently gross (division by zero, overflow, underflow), so the hardware warns the user of trouble.

Most of the trouble occurs because real numbers are stored only with a limited number of digits. The result of calculations can be disastrous even in logically correct programs that have been used with no noticeable error for a long period of time. A new set of input may produce obviously incorrect results. The problem is because the computer uses only a set precision for real numbers. For example:

```
A = 1.0/3.0        Provides the value 0.3333333
.
.
.
B = A*3            Provides the value 0.9999999
```

The unwary programmer may use the above in a logical test as follows:

$$IF \ (B = 1) \ ...$$

Another serious error can be caused by

$$I = B$$

where I is an integer and B is real with the value 0.9999999. The result stored in I will be zero because of integer truncation.

LOCATING ERRORS

Locating an error in a program is often quite difficult. Some of the reasons for wanting to locate an error are:

1. Not sure if the program started to execute.
2. The program started to execute but terminated prematurely, either with or without a system error.

3. The program started to execute but got caught in an endless loop, as indicated by the program taking too long.
4. The program provided incorrect answers.

Any of these errors requires the programmer to trace the flow through the program. There are usually TRACE statements available to do this, but there are disadvantages with TRACE statements that are mentioned in the section on debugging aids.

Locating an unknown place in a program is basically setting up a search strategy. In some cases (for example, when a systems error message is the only output) there is little knowledge of where the error is in the program. Otherwise, the programmer has some knowledge (for example, when some output is available) of where the error is. If the exact location of the error is known, then it is normally simple to correct the error.

The goal is to keep narrowing down the error location until found. Thus, parts of the program may have a zero probability of the error being there while other sections of the program may have a high probability of containing the error. The goal is to find the error, that is, to increase the probability of finding the location of the error until it is 100%.

The general method for tracing your own program is to put between 5 and 10 output statements in the program. One output statement should be at the beginning of the program and another at the end of the program. The rest of the output statements should be spaced at fairly regular intervals throughout the program.

It is best to avoid putting debug statements inside loops. Instead, put the debug output statements immediately before and after loops. If debugging output statements are put inside loops they will produce output each time the loop is executed which could easily be thousands of times.

My favorite output statement for tracing program flow is to print statements as follows:

```
DEBUG 1
DEBUG 2
```

That is, the first debug statement should print the word DEBUG plus the number 1. The next debug statement will print DEBUG and the number 2. The word DEBUG indicates that it is a debugging statement and is to be removed after debugging is complete.

Once these statements are placed in the program, the position of the error is easy to locate.

Suppose we had placed 10 debug statements interspersed throughout the program. Then our output might look as follows:

```
DEBUG 1
DEBUG 2
DEBUG 3
DEBUG 4
```

Since DEBUG 4 is the last statement printed, we know the error is between the statement that prints DEBUG 4 and the statement that prints DEBUG 5. If inspection of these statements does not produce the error, then one can take all 10 debug statements and put them in the program between the statements where DEBUG 4 and DEBUG 5 were. The process will eventually lead to the error.

If the above debugging statements are kept after they are removed from the program they can be used again in other programs. Thus one can develop his own standard debugging package which can be used in a wide variety of programs.

Once you find the error statement, you are often not finished. The statement that causes the error is usually elsewhere. For example:

$$C = B/A$$

This statement would cause trouble when A had the value zero. So the next step is to trace the previous statement to determine why A has the value zero.

Thus, when locating an error, there are two considerations: *point of detection* and *point of origin*. The point of detection is the location where the error manifested itself or where it became apparent. This is the first point that must be located. In the above example, the point of detection is the above statement.

The point of origin is the location where the error condition was created; that is, in the above example, where A assumed the value zero. The real error takes place at the original point, not the detection point. The detection point is just the starting point in the search for the error origin point.

DEBUGGING OUTPUT

Debugging output are statements that are used to print results of calculations for debugging purposes. The first debugging statements needed are the echo-printing of all input data. Next, information is needed that will indicate the progress of numeric calculations. Finally, output statements are needed that will indicate the logic flow of the program.

If large amounts of computations are involved, a wrong answer will seldom provide enough information to locate the error. Variables that are printed out during debugging should be clearly labeled so it is evident which variables are being printed. It should not be considered unusual to have a great deal of the program devoted to debugging aids. And all the debugging aids put in the source program should be designed so their removal will not cause bugs in the program. Since it is common to compile a program 20 or 30 times while debugging, it pays to provide debugging output early to reduce the number of compiles necessary.

The aids actually provided by the programmer are usually the most helpful and effective. It is usually easier to put these aids in while writing the program than to add them later during the debugging stage. It is trivial to remove debugging aids once the program is completely debugged and tested.

It is typical not to introduce enough debugging aids at the writing stage. This is because one really never knows how necessary these aids will be until completely bogged down at the debugging stage. A good question for deciding if debugging statements are needed is: If the program is incorrect, in this block of coding will there be enough output to locate the errors?

One forgets that more programmer time is spent at the debugging stage than at all other stages. And on many programs more machine time is spent debugging than even on the production runs.

Debugging aids that are built into the original program are called *bug arresting*. They are used to preserve the evidence that permits bug identification by locating the specific fault. The usual approach to debugging is to discover an obvious bug and then attempt to backtrack. But there is usually no trail to backtrack. So one must put in several debugging runs to attempt to locate the bugs.

Strategically placed output statements will provide both an arithmetic and a flow trace of what happened during the execution of the program. Generally, the earlier a number of debugging statements can be put into the program, the less the number of debugging runs that will be required.

After debugging is completed, all the debugging statements must be eliminated. The best method of elimination is to change them to comments to suppress output. Then the debugging statements will be available if needed later. Otherwise, if a bug appears later or a program modification is required, the debugging statements would not normally be available. By changing the debugging statements into comments they are carried along with the program as documentation and are readily available.

If you are using a terminal system, it is possible to label the debugging and testing lines so the editing system can automatically remove these lines. For example, if you were using FORTRAN, you could start all lines you want to remove with statement numbers 9XXXX. Then direct the editing system to remove these lines.

Finally, if the test lines are changed to comments they provide an important part of the documentation, indicating the specific tests which were done.

IBM PL/I allows the programmer to specify the left and right margins for program source statements by using the SORMGIN option. The normal margins, when using card input, are SORMGIN=(2,72). This margin feature can be used to switch a program from the debugging/testing version to the production version automatically.

Here's how. Use SORMGIN=(4,70) for the debugging and testing version of the source program. Use SORMGIN=(2,72) for the production version. Then, for all debugging and testing statements that you wish removed before production use, just place the /* in columns 2-3 and a */ in columns 71-72. Since these are the comment delimiters, this allows automatic conversion of debugging and testing statements to comments.

SELECTIVE PRINTOUT

Often it is desirable to selectively print some information during debugging. This situation arises when only certain cases are to be checked, or when a nonselective printout would provide too much output, such as putting a print statement within a loop.

An example of a statement to do selective printing is:

```
IF (X .LT. 0.0) WRITE ...
```

This statement would print out data only when X is less than zero. The following could be used to check an index and selectively print debugging information:

```
IF (I .GT. 10 .AND. I .LT. 15) WRITE ...
```

This statement would provide printout only when $I = 11, 12, 13,$ or 14.

The following example takes advantage of integer arithmetic.

```
IF (I / 5 * 5 - I .EQ. 0) WRITE ...
```

The expression

```
I / 5 * 5 - I
```

will equal zero only when I has a 5 as a factor (that is, $I = 5, 10,$ $15, \ldots$) because of integer arithmetic. This technique can be used to print data every nth iteration.

Selective printouts can also be used to check to see how many iterations are taken on iterative routines as follows:

```
IF ( N .EQ. 1000 ) WRITE ...
```

This statement will indicate when N has reached 1,000 which may indicate an infinite loop. The above statement is much safer than putting a nonconditional output statement inside a loop.

A very useful type of statement is:

```
IF DEBUGGING THEN ...
```

where DEBUGGING is a logical variable with either a true or false value. This type of construct allows you to turn your debugging (or testing) statements on or off for the whole program by setting just one logical variable to true or false. If this method is used, debugging statements can be left in the program for later possible use. Just set DEBUGGING to false.

LOGIC TRACES

Output statements can be used to indicate the flow of execution in the program. This type of output statement is usually put in subroutines or after program decisions are made. Thus, the completion of the various stages of the program will be recorded by printing suitable chosen messages. An example of output might be:

```
ENTERED SUBROUTINE MAXNUM.
EXITED SUBROUTINE MAXNUM.
ENTERED SUBROUTINE FIXNUM.
LESS THAN ZERO BRANCH TAKEN.
ONE THOUSAND ITERATIONS.
```

The first three output comments indicate which subroutines are being executed. The fourth comment indicates a particular branch was taken. The last output comment indicates how many iterations have been executed. Output statements should indicate both desirable and undesirable conditions.

Debugging output statements can be easily removed when the program is accepted as correct or changed to comments so they can be used later if needed. It is usually easier to include these debugging statements when the program is being written than to wait until the program has been tried and found to fail. Logic flow statements will help the programmer discover bugs that might stay hidden otherwise.

One very simple aid to debugging that is often overlooked is that all programs should print out a final message indicating that the program reached normal completion. Just before stopping execution print:

```
NORMAL END OF JOB.
```

Otherwise, it is easy to overlook the fact that the program did not complete execution.

ERROR CHECKLIST

Most programmers have certain errors in coding which they tend to make over and over. This may be using illegal subscripts, writing conditional jumps the wrong way, or counting from one when counting should start at zero, etc. These types of errors are particularly common if one habitually programs in two or more languages. Since each language works differently, it is easy to confuse them. What you should do is keep a list of your own common errors. This list can then be used as a checklist while debugging. Tables 4.2 and 4.3 list many common programming errors.

Table 4.2 A Catalog of Bugs (A classification of bugs by type)

These are not syntax errors, but bugs that would still be present after syntax checking is complete.

Logic
1. Taking the wrong path at a logic decision.
2. Failure to consider one or more conditions.
3. Omission of coding one or more flowchart boxes.
4. Branching to the wrong label.

Loops
1. Not initializing the loop properly.
2. Not terminating the loop properly.
3. Wrong number of loop cycles.
4. Incorrect indexing of the loop.
5. Infinite loops (sometimes called closed loops).

Data
1. Failure to consider all possible data types.
2. Failure to edit out incorrect data.
3. Trying to read less or more data than there are.
4. Editing data incorrectly or mismatching of editing fields with data fields.

Variables
1. Using an uninitialized variable.
2. Not resetting a counter or accumulator.
3. Failure to set a program switch correctly.
4. Using an incorrect variable name (that is, spelling error using wrong variable).

Arrays
1. Failure to clear the array.
2. Failure to declare arrays large enough.
3. Transpose the subscript order.

Table 4.2 (cont'd.)

Arithmetic Operations (see also Variables)
1. Using wrong mode (that is, using integer when real was needed).
2. Overflow and underflow.
3. Using incorrect constant.
4. Evaluation order incorrect.
5. Division by zero.
6. Squareroot of a negative value.
7. Truncation.

Subroutines
1. Incorrect attributes of function.
2. Incorrect attributes of subroutine parameters.
3. Incorrect number of parameters.

Input/Output (see also Data)
1. Incorrect mode of I/O format specifications.
2. Failure to rewind (or position) a tape before reading or writing.
3. Using wrong size records or incorrect formats.

Character Strings
1. Declare character string the wrong size.
2. Attempting to reference a character outside the range of the string length.

Logical Operations
1. Using the wrong logical operator.
2. Comparing variables which do not have compatible attributes.
3. Failure to provide ELSE clause in multiple IF statements.

Machine Operations
1. Incorrect shifting.
2. Using an incorrect machine constant (that is, using decimal when hexadecimal was needed).

Terminators
1. Failure to terminate a statement.
2. Failure to terminate a comment.
3. Using " instead of ' , or vice versa.
4. Incorrectly matched quote.
5. Terminate prematurely.

Miscellaneous
1. Not abiding by statement margin restrictions.
2. Using wrong function.

Table 4.3 Special Bugs

There is another category of bugs that I will call special bugs. These are sophisticated errors (that is, difficult to locate).

Semantic Error
These errors are caused by the failure to understand exactly how a command works. An example is to assume that arithmetic operations are rounded. Another example is to assume that a loop will be skipped if the

Table 4.3 (cont'd.)

ending value is smaller than the initial value. In IBM FORTRAN DO, loops are always executed once.

Semaphore Bug

This type of bug becomes evident when process A is waiting upon a process B while process B is waiting upon process A. This type of bug usually emerges when running large complicated systems such as operating systems.

Timing Bug

A *timing bug* can develop when two operations depend on each other in a time sense. That is, operation A must be completed before operation B can start. If operation B starts too soon, a timing bug can appear. Both timing bugs and semaphore bugs are called *situation bugs*.

Operation Irregularity Bugs

These bugs are the result of machine operations. Sometimes unsuspecting programmers do not understand that the machine does arithmetic in binary, so the innocent expression

$$1.0/5.0*5.0$$

does not equal one. This error shows up when this test is made:

```
A = 5.0
    .
    .
    .
B = 5.0
    .
    .
    .
IF (1.0/A*B .EQ. 1.0) . . .
```

Then an unexpected branch takes place, and probably an endless loop results.

Evanescent Bug

Another bug that doesn't usually appear until production phase is the *evanescent bug*. This is a bug that appears and then may disappear for several months. This includes the bugs that will not reappear even when identical data and program are rerun through the same machine. An example of a bug of this type is a program switch that has not been initialized, but usually is correct due to the tendency of the machine to have a zero in that particular location.

Another variation is when debugging tools are added, the bugs disappear. The author once spent two months trying to locate this type of bug and failed. My solution was to rewrite the program.

PROGRAM DIMENSIONS

In debugging there are two dimensions to be traced: space and time. The space dimension is storage space in the computer. The time dimension is the computation cycles completed during execution. Usually, the time dimension is the longest and most important. Debugging aids concentrate on allowing the programmer to trace both dimensions. Debugging aids are stethoscopes necessary to isolate the cause and location of an error.

DEBUGGING AIDS

A repertoire of debugging aids is a welcome source of help during debugging. But they seldom relieve the programmer from constructing his own debugging aids. The most effective debugging aids seem to be those that are written into the program while writing the original program. That is because the error areas can be pinpointed by the programmer.

There are several debugging programming aids. They are usually:

1. dumps
2. flow trace
3. variable trace
4. subroutine trace
5. subscript checks
6. display

A *dump* is a record of information at a given time of the status of the program. This is usually provided in machine language and is of limited use for several reasons. The major reason is because it is difficult to relate the dump to your program. It requires the programmer to understand machine language and to be able to relate the machine language to his high-level language. In addition, if the compiler optimizes high-level code, it becomes even more difficult to use the dump even if machine language is known. A highly optimizing compiler may entirely rearrange the operations in a program, thus making a dump almost useless. Since the information provided in a dump is not in a form where it can be used, there has been a trend to provide debugging aids that give debugging information in a form more appropriate for use. The paper by Gaines cited in the references discusses different types of dumps.

A *trace* is a record of the path of execution of the program. It can be used to see if the program is being executed in the same sequence as the programmer intended, and if the variables have the desired values stored in them. There are usually three types of traces. The first type traces the flow of control of the program. That is, it usually prints statement labels as they are passed during execution.

The second type of trace prints variable names and values. Every time a variable changes in value, the variable label and its new value are printed.

A third type traces subroutine calls. This becomes very useful in a program that calls many subroutines. Every time a subroutine is called, the name of the subroutine is printed; and when a return from the subroutine is executed, a return message prints.

Traces will often provide all the information needed to locate a bug in a program. But their weakness is that they can easily provide too much information, that is, thousands of lines of output. The second disadvantage is that, because of the great amount of information monitored and provided, they are usually quite costly in machine time. A full trace can easily increase execution time by a factor of 10 to 40 times.

Thus, in order to overcome the above difficulties, flow traces are usually designed so they can be turned on and off. That is, they can be turned on just for the section of the program that needs to be traced and turned off for the other sections.

Variable traces are designed so that, instead of printing out all variables, only a selected list of variables is monitored and printed.

ALGOL W has some very sophisticated tracing options. Here are a few:

1. A post-mortem dump of all the program's variables if execution terminates abnormally, else nothing.
2. The above plus counts of how often each statement was executed.
3. The above plus a statement-by-statement trace of each value stored.
4. The above plus a trace of each value fetched.

In addition, a logic trace or trace of flow of control can be requested.   An upper limit can be set on the maximum number of times any statement is to be traced. That is, if an upper bound of 4 is requested, no statement will be traced more than 4 times. The postmortem dump may seem unexceptional until we note that all debugging outputs are in terms of the source language. All variables are given by the same name and format as declared, branches are given in terms of program labels, and, in statement tracing, the original source statements, as well as the values of the pertinent variables, are printed out as each is executed.

A *subscript* check monitors the validity of all subscripts used with the named arrays by comparing the subscript combination with the declared bounds of the array. If the subscript falls outside the declared range, an error message is printed. It is usually possible to monitor all or just some arrays.

A *display* debugging command allows the user to select the exact place in the program when the variable value is to be printed. This allows a much more selective printing than the variable trace. In addition, the display command usually prints the variable name along with the variable value. This provides labeled output automatically.

MODULES FOR CHECKING PROGRAMS

Occasionally a module can be used to help debug a program. If elaborate printing of variables is desired, a module can be used at several places in a program to provide this. Use of a debugging module also simplifies the removal of debugging statements. Special debugging modules are often useful when testing out single modules before they are combined.

AUTOMATIC CHECKS

During debugging, many of the possible automatic checks should be used.   This includes division by zero, arithmetic overflow, arithmetic underflow, string range, and subscript range checks. Some compilers allow these options to be turned off or on because they require considerable execution time. The above checks, besides indicating a specific error, often indicate a serious logic error.

TIME NEEDED FOR DEBUGGING

One tends continually to underestimate the time needed for debugging. Here is a formula I have used. Figure out how much time is needed for programming, double it, and call it one unit. Then a projected timetable might be:

Task	Units
Planning	1
Writing	1
Debugging	4
Testing	1

It is generally agreed that debugging always takes the most time. The question is: How much more? Try this schedule and see how it works. Then adjust it to your own needs. If you are able to reduce the debugging time but your program continually blows up during production runs, then you are cheating.

PREVENTING BUGS

Debugging is often the largest program development cost. Thus effort should be made to prevent bugs. There are a few rules that, if followed, will help eliminate some bugs.

Avoid questionable coding. Assume advance features won't work unless you know they work. Use the simplest statements. Don't try to fool the compiler or the system. Compilers and operating systems are very complicated and it is not unusual to find a loophole in one where you can violate a language syntax rule and still get correct results. The only problem is, since you did violate the syntax rule, the computer manufacturer is under no duress to allow your trick to work on future releases or updates of the computer language or operating system. So an operational program with tricky coding in it may easily not run under new releases of the language. This type of bug can be very difficult to find a year or two after you wrote the original program.

Avoid dependence on defaults. All programming languages have some language defaults which the compiler assumes. The use of these defaults saves work for the programmer, but can be dangerous because computer manufacturers occasionally change the defaults. In addition, the programmer may assume a wrong default is being used. IBM changed a default size for one variable type in PL/I on one of its frequent language releases and many PL/I programs became inoperable. Also, different machines have different defaults, and if it is desirable to maintain portability of your program, it is best to avoid using too many defaults.

Never allow data dependency. Never allow your program to depend upon whether the input data is in a special form or within a restricted range. Instead, check the data at input time to make sure they are correct. Data always follow Murphy's law: "Anything that can go wrong will." Data errors can be caused by ignoring input instructions, keypunch errors, or input/output errors. If data are not checked at input, the program will periodically be found to have mysteriously blown up. After laboriously tracing the error it will be found that it was the fault of the input data. But the program and the programmer will still gain a reputation of unreliability.

Always complete your logic decisions. If data are to have a 1 or 2 code, don't check for a 1 and, if false, assume a 2. This overlooks the pathological cases that will often be present. Always check for the 1; then if not true, check for the 2. If neither 1 nor 2, then program the pathological case, that is, usually an error message or halt.

CONCLUSION

The listings of possible errors in this chapter will probably not teach anyone how to debug a program, but they can be used as a checklist of what to check next when you are stuck while debugging. This might be called the entomology of program bugs: the study of bugs by observation.

The principle approach to debugging is to provide enough information in printed form so the program error can be easily located. The expert programmer knows where to put his debugging statements, while the beginning programmer has no idea where to start and thus uses a great deal of his time and the machine's time debugging. It is a rare program that doesn't need any debugging statements.

As Gruenberger nicely puts it: "When debugging is completed the program definitely solves some problem." The next chapter on testing is to ensure that the program solves the problem that was intended.

EXERCISES

1. Survey the lists of errors in this chapter to see how many you are familiar with.

2. Build a list of programming errors you continually run into.

3. Discuss the advantages and disadvantages of the debugging techniques included in this chapter.

4. What are some other debugging techniques besides the ones mentioned in this chapter?

5. When should a TRACE be used and when should you write your own trace statements?

6. What debugging aids would you like? How many of these are available to you?

7. What checks (like checking subscripts) would you like your compiler to develop code for during execution?

8. Which of the following debugging aids on your compiler are available?
   (a) flow trace
   (b) turn flow trace off and on
   (c) variable trace
   (d) selective variable trace
   (e) subroutine call trace
   (f) dumps
   (f) a display command that labels output with variable names

9. What are some of the reasons subroutines simplify debugging?

10. If your compiler has a subscript range checker, would it detect an error for $A(4,2)$ if the array was declared with dimensions $A(3,4)$?

11. Is there a debugging compiler available for the programming language you code in? Does it offer enough advantages that it would be worth obtaining?

12. If you use a language that has blocks (that is, DO, BEGIN), does the compiler indicate the level of nesting for the blocks?

13. Develop a personal list of error messages and their probable cause while working on your own programs. Here are two examples:

Error Message	Probable Cause
Time exceeded	Infinite loop
Overflow	Undefined variable

14. Look at Table 4.1. Is the table complete? Can you think of any changes that should be made?

15. Using Table 4.2 as a starting point, add to the catalog of bugs to develop your own personal catalog.

16. In this chapter I listed a few errors that the compiler cannot detect. Think of at least five other types of errors the compiler cannot detect.

17. What are the space dimension and the time dimension in a program? How is each dimension traced when debugging?

18. Which of the following checks are done during compilation by the compiler you use?
    (a) sequence check source decks
    (b) unused labels
    (c) unused statements
    (d) unused variables
    (e) truncation in moves
    (f) statement which transfers to itself
    (g) transfer into the middle of a DO (FOR) loop
    (h) variable type and format specification match
    (i) function arguments wrong type

(j)   attempt to use a nonrecursive subprogram recursively

(k)   attempt to use a subroutine as a function or vice versa

(l)   incorrect number of subscripts

(m) illegal bit strings

(n)   correct attributes in comparisons

(o)   assignment compatibility

Arrange the above checks in order of importance to you. What other checks would you like done by your compiler? Would it be logically possible to provide these checks?

19. Which of the following checks are provided during execution by the compiler you use?

(a)   using an uninitialized variable

(b)   illegal subscript

(c)   real overflow

(d)   real underflow

(e)   integer overflow

(f)   exponent overflow

(g)   exponent underflow

(h)   division by zero

(i)   indetermine, that is, $0**0$

(j)   correct number of subroutine arguments

(k)   correct attributes of subroutine arguments

(l)   character string range errors

(m) conversion errors

(n)   bound checks on statements where bounds are critical

Arrange the above checks in order of importance to you. What other checks would you like provided by your compiler? Would it be logically possible to provide these checks?

20. Does your compiler provide the following options for debugging?

(a)   list all variables in alphabetic order (*storage map*)

(b)   list all constants used

(c)   list of variables showing attributes (*attribute table*)

(d)   list of functions used

(e)   list of subroutines used

(f)   list each variable indicating all statements which use it (*cross-reference table*)

(g)   list all statements which reference each label

Arrange the above options in order of importance to you. What other options would you like to have available? Would it be logically possible to provide these options?

21. Write a small program (less than 50 lines of code). Have a contest with others to see who can generate the most compiler error messages in one program.

22. Write a small program (less than 50 lines of code) that will compile successfully with no syntax errors, but will force the program to abnormally abort before execution is completed. A trivial technique to do this would be to cause a division by zero. How many different ways can you get your program to abort during execution?

23. Take the above program and give it to someone else and have that person find the error.

24. Take a small program and modify the program in a subtle manner so the answer is obviously incorrect. Then trade it with someone else and see if that person can find your error.

25. Set up a bulletin board and post programs in which errors are difficult to locate so others can try to find them.

26. What is the difference between syntax errors and execution errors? List seven syntax errors and seven execution errors.

27. Write a small program and misspell some of the reserved words. How many different types of error messages can you create this way?

28. Write a program that uses an array but does not declare the array. How many different types of error messages appear? Do any of the error messages indicate the problem?

29. Write a program to obtain as many *different* compiler error messages as possible. Next, classify the types of error messages. For example:
    (a) The error is discovered and error message correctly identifies the error.
    (b) The error is discovered, but a misleading error message is printed.
    (c) No error is present, but an error message occurs.
    Are there any obvious errors that do not produce error messages?

30. Use logical statements to test the following comparisons on your computer. Use real values for X and Y.
    (a) Does $X^0 = X^{0.0} = 1$ for all X?
    (b) Does $\mathsf{SQRT}(X) = X^{0.5} = X^{(1.0/2.0)}$ for all X?
    (c) Does $X = X^1 = X^{1.0}$ for all X?
    (d) Does $X*X = X^2 = X^{2.0}$ for all X?
    (e) Does $X*X*X = X^3 = X^{3.0}$ for all X?
    (f) Does $X/Y*Y = X$ for all X, Y?
    (g) Does $\sin^2 X + \cos^2 X = 1$ for all X?

    (h) Does $1000*(1.0/5.0) = \displaystyle\sum_{i=1}^{1000} \left(\frac{1.0}{5.0}\right)$?

    Think of some other "logically true" statements to check.

31. Write a program to do the following:

    $$Y = A + B + C$$

    where $A = -2,500,000.00$, $B = 0.01$, $C = 2,500,001.00$. Is the answer correct? If not, why? Could you rearrange the calculation so it would be correct?

32. Use logical statements to test the following comparisons on your computer. Use real values for A, B, and C.
    (a) Does $A + B - A = B$ for all A, B?
    (b) Does $A(B - C) = AB - AC$ for all A, B, C?
    (c) Does $\dfrac{A - B}{C} = A/C - B/C$ for all A, B, C?
    (d) Does $(A + B) + C = A + (B + C)$ for all A, B, C?

33. Pretend you wish to redesign a computer so $X = Y$ is *true* not only for exact equality, but also when the two values differ only in the least significant digit represented. Do you think this would be a good idea? If you did the above, does

    $$a = b \quad \text{and} \quad b = c \quad \text{imply that} \quad a = c?$$

    Give some examples where equality will occur under the above conditions. Give some examples where equality will not occur under the above conditions.

34. Write a program to do each of the following:
     (a) Sum 0.1 ten times.
     (b) Sum 0.01 one hundred times.
     (c) Sum 0.001 one thousand times.
     (d) Sum 0.0001 ten thousand times.
     (e) Sum 0.000001 one million times.
     Print the maximum significant digits. How close are the results
     to unity? Why are some results not exact?

35. Program the evaluation of $\sum_{n=1}^{100} \dfrac{1}{n^3}$ by adding forward and also

     by adding backward. Which sum is likely to be nearest the
     exact answer?

36. There are many mathematical functions that have an inverse
     function available. But, because of truncation error, sometimes
     the inverse operation does not provide the original value. Write
     a program to see if the following functions will always return
     the original value for random values of X.

     (a) $Y = SQRT(X)$ then $X = Y*Y$
     (b) $Y = LOG(X)$ then $X = EXP(Y)$
     (c) $Y = SIN(X)$ then $X = ARSIN(Y)$
     (d) $Y = COS(X)$ then $X = ARCOS(Y)$

     Can you think of any other functions to test this way? In each
     of the above can you notice any trend? That is, do large num-
     bers (or numbers near PI) produce more problems than small
     numbers, or vice versa?

37. Write a program to evaluate each of these sums:

     (a) $1 - \dfrac{1}{2} + \dfrac{1}{3} - \dfrac{1}{4} + \dfrac{1}{5} - \cdots - \dfrac{1}{10000}$

     (b) $-\dfrac{1}{10000} + \dfrac{1}{9999} - \dfrac{1}{9998} + \cdots - \dfrac{1}{2} + 1$

     (c) $(1 + \dfrac{1}{3} + \dfrac{1}{5} + \cdots + \dfrac{1}{9999}) - (\dfrac{1}{2} + \dfrac{1}{4} + \dfrac{1}{6} + \cdots + \dfrac{1}{10000})$

     (d) $(\dfrac{1}{9999} + \dfrac{1}{9997} + \cdots + \dfrac{1}{3} + 1) - (\dfrac{1}{10000} + \dfrac{1}{9998} + \cdots$

     $+ \dfrac{1}{4} + \dfrac{1}{2})$

Notice that all the above are the same sums. Why do the answers differ? Which answer is correct?

38. Real constants must be converted from base 10 to machine base before being stored. On some compilers, different results will occur between read constants and set constants when too many significant digits are involved. Try a program similar to the following:

Any Language

```
A1 = 1111111111.111
READ   A2
WRITE   A1, A2
END
$DATA
1111111111.111
```

Write a program similar to the above and try different large values. Are the results printed for A1 and A2 always the same?

39. When using subroutines, one particularly nasty bug presents itself in various languages. Here is a FORTRAN example:

FORTRAN

```
        CALL SUBA (2,K)
        WRITE (6,10) K
        I = 2
        WRITE (6,10) I
10      FORMAT (1X,I5)
        STOP
        END
        SUBROUTINE  SUBA(L, M)
        L = L+L
        M = L
        RETURN
        END
```

(a) Trace through the program and figure out what values will print out.
(b) Punch the program and submit it to run. Does the answer you thought should print, actually print?
(c) If the answer is different than the expected answer, what happened? How can you prevent this type of bug?

40. Here is a program and the printed results.
    (a) Trace through the program and figure out what the results should be. Is the printed result correct?
    (b) If not, why not? If you cannot find the error, keypunch the program and debug it.

```
FACTOR: PROCEDURE OPTIONS (MAIN);
 /* FIND FACTORIAL OF 5 */
    FACT: PROCEDURE(N) RECURSIVE;
         IF N>1 THEN RETURN (N*FACT(N-1));
                ELSE RETURN(1);
    END FACT;

    M = 5;
    X = FACT(M);
    PUT DATA(X);
END FACTOR;
```

Printed Result:

$$X = 5.00000E+00;$$

41. An assignment statement that would assign two different values simultaneously to the same variable would be undesirable. It might look like the following:

$$(A,A) = (2,3)$$

Can you think of ways to do this in your programming language? Here is one way:

```
          CALL  SUBA (A,B,A)
          PRINT A
          STOP
          END
          SUBROUTINE  SUBA (X,Y,Z)
                X = 1.0
                Y = 2.0
                Z = 3.0
                RETURN
          END
```

What value do you expect will print from the above code? Program the above in your favorite programming language.

42. What value will print from the following program?

```
      A = 2
      CALL SUBA(A,A)
      WRITE(6,10) A
10    FORMAT(1X, ' A=', F5.1)
      STOP
      END

      SUBROUTINE SUBA(A,B)
        A = A + B**3
        IF ( A .LT. SQRT(B) ) B = 5.15
        RETURN
      END
```

If you cannot agree on the result, program the problem in your favorite programming language.

43. Here is a program and the printed results.
   (a) Trace through the program and figure out what the results should be. Is the printed result correct?
   (b) If not, why not? If you cannot find the error, keypunch the program and debug it.

```
LOOP: PROCEDURE OPTIONS (MAIN);
    DECLARE X(10) DECIMAL FLOAT;
    DO Y = 0.1 TO 1.0 BY 0.1;
        I = 10*Y;
        X(I) = Y;
    END;
    PUT EDIT ((X(I) DO I = 1 TO 10)) (SKIP, F(8,2));
END LOOP;
```

Printed Result:

```
               0.20
               0.30
               0.40
               0.50
               0.60
               0.70
               0.80
               0.90
               1.00
           29312.00
```

44. *Limits of Your Compiler.* Many commands within your compiler have limitations. These limits are usually so large that you will seldom encounter them. For example, one popular compiler will allow about 400 parentheses in *one* statement before objecting. An interesting exercise is to find other limitations on your favorite compiler. Here are some suggestions:
    (a) Maximum number of parentheses in one statement.
    (b) Maximum size of a 1-dimensional array. Maximum dimensions of an array.
    (c) Maximum length of literal or bit constant.
    (d) Maximum length of a single statement.
    (e) Maximum length comment or maximum number of consecutive comments.
    (f) Maximum number of nested DO loops (or blocks or IF THEN ELSE).
    (g) Maximum number of subroutines (or nested calls to subroutines).
    (h) Maximum number of arguments in a subroutine.
    (i) Maximum number of recursive calls.
    Can you think of any other restrictions of this type? Hint: Try examining the list of error messages for your language compiler.

REFERENCES

Barron, D. W. "Programming in Wonderland," *Computer Bulletin.* 15, 1971.

Bemer, Robert W. "Economics of Program Production," *Datamation.* September, 1966.

Brown, A. R., and W. A. Sampson. *Program Debugging.* New York: American Elsevier. 1973.

Fong, Elizabeth N. "Improving Compiler Diagnostics," *Datamation.* April, 1973.

Gaines, R. Stockton. *The Debugging of Computer Programs.* Institute for Defense Analysis, Princeton, N.J. August, 1969.

Halpern, Mark. "Computer Programming: The Debugging Epoch Opens," *Computers and Automation.* November, 1965.

Henry, R. W. *Standards in Program Development.* The Institute for Advanced Technology. Control Data Corporation. 1971.

IEEE Symposium on Computer Software Reliability. 1973. IEEE Computer Society. New York.

Poole, P. C. "Debugging and Testing," *Advanced Course in Software Engineering.* New York: Springer-Verlag, 1973.

Rustin, Randall, Editor. *Debugging Techniques in Large Systems.* Englewood Cliffs, N.J.: Prentice-Hall, Inc. 1971.

Rustin, Randall, Editor. *Debugging Techniques in Large Systems,* 1971. Englewood Cliffs, N.J.: Prentice-Hall, Inc.

Satterthwaite, E. "Debugging Tools for High Level Languages," *Software-Practice and Experience.* Vol. 2, 1972.

Sherman, Philip M. *Programming and Coding Digital Computers,* Englewood Cliffs, N.J.: Prentice-Hall, Inc. 1970.

Sherman, Philip M. *Techniques in Computer Programming,* Englewood Cliffs, N.J.: Prentice-Hall, Inc.

Walter, Arline B., and Marilyn Bohl. "From Better to Best Tips for Good Programming," *Software Age.* November, 1969.

Zolnowsky, John. "Debugging Facilities: A Review." Research Report for CS390. Stanford University. January, 1971.

Testing shows the presence,
not the absence of bugs.   Dijkstra

Testing should be a consideration
throughout the entire development
of the program.

V

Program Testing

If program testing is conducted in a laissez-faire manner where the tester rambles around with no set direction, then program testing is an art. If the program tester carefully selects the required test data, carefully plots the points to be tested, and carefully executes the tests, then program testing is a science.

Planning and coding a program are skills that can be learned. Then it is time for program testing to shift from testing as an art to testing as a science.

If the laissez-faire approach to program testing is used, there is no way to prevent duplicate testing, no way to control testing so the areas with the highest payoffs are covered, no way to evaluate how complete the testing is, no way to determine when testing is completed.

Testing is a distinct step from debugging. Debugging is the removing of syntax errors and obviously incorrect coding. Once these are removed and the program produces some correct results, then the testing stage commences. The main reason for insisting that there are two separate steps is to insure that both steps are done and that both steps have time allotted to them.

You must never assume the program is correct just because it is accepted by the computer, completely compiled, and numerical results achieved. All you have done here is obtain some results—not necessarily the correct results. Many logic errors may still exist. The requirement is not to produce answers, but to produce *correct* answers. Thus, you must usually check out the results by hand calculations. Once all debugging is completed, even the experienced programmer will still have an error for every 20 or 30 statements written. These errors can range from the catastrophic to the trivial—from complete errors in logic to small coding errors.

SPECIFICATION VERSUS PROGRAM TESTING

Program testing is the process of guaranteeing that the program works in all cases in which it is supposed to work. Two types of testing should take place. First, the testing must prove that the problem specified was programmed. Second, we must test to learn whether the program works correctly.

Specification testing is impossible if the problem specifications are not complete, clear, and consistent. It must be completely stated what results are to be obtained over the input domain. Clearness means that all parties must understand what is to be accomplished. Consistency means no ambiguities are allowed. If the program specifications are complete, clear, and consistent, a program tester can treat the program as a "black box" (without knowing anything about the coding) and test the final program.

Some testing can be done before any of the program is coded. This is simply a "hand simulation" of the logic of the specifications. Some errors may be discovered in this way before coding has started and thus be easy to correct.

BEGINNING PROGRAMMERS

Beginning programmers do not realize programs are wrong until proven correct. An untested program usually is a source of future embarrassment when it produces obviously incorrect results. Then, if the program has been used and believed for a period of time, all previous results of the program are of questionable veracity. This is when the programmer learns that he never tested the program, only debugged it. Amateur programmers work on a program until it provides results, but not always correct results, then the program is abandoned for a new project.

ROBUSTNESS

The goal of program testing is to ensure that the program solves the problem that it is supposed to solve, and that it yields the correct answer under all conditions. The latter is usually called the *durability* or *robustness* of a program. A program that stops producing correct results easily is not durable or robust. Programs tend to become more robust the longer they are used because, as they are used, failures are discovered and corrected.

A program can appear to work for months and even years before it will be apparent that there is a major error in some part of it. There is a theory that big programs are never completely error-free. Testing should never be skimped to save money or time. An incorrect program is worth less than no program at all, because of the false conclusions it produces.

It may inspire others to make expensive errors. The expense of reprocessing a year's transactions because of an incompletely tested program will forcefully demonstrate that adequate testing is desirable.

While it is impossible in an exact sense to specify completely how to test programs, there are a number of hints and guidelines that will aid in the task of program testing. This chapter is devoted to discussing these testing techniques.

GENERAL HINTS

The most important hint about program testing is that some thought should go into the testing phase while the program is being written. Constant attention should be paid to the question: "How will I test this segment?" If you write a routine and you don't know how you will ever test it, the routine should be rewritten or broken into modules. The ultimate result of a program which is difficult to test is that it is never completely tested, and sooner or later it will fail during a production run.

Once all test cases have been used and proved successful, real data should be used. Real data will uncover many errors that test data will fail to locate. Here is a suggested minimum list of successful tests:

Each Module	4 runs
Complete Program	4 runs
Live Data	3 runs
System Test	2 runs

On complex programs the above numbers will probably be inadequate.

Programs should be reassembled for each test, immediately prior to the test. Object decks should not be used because source code will usually be in a state of flux. Use of object decks can easily lead to confusion because it is difficult to ascertain which object deck matches which source version.

Consider having someone else test your program. This is especially true if the program is very complex. A fresh point of view will often uncover errors that the original programmer will miss because of too much familiarity with the program.

If cards have to be added to the source program to aid testing, punch them on a different color from the rest of the program. Also keypunch TEST in columns 73–80 of each test card. Then you will have two reminders to remove these test source cards.

Control over the quality of the code produced should be established early. The code should be checked by experienced personnel to detect loose code, poor programming practices, and deviation from program specifications. Early catching of potential errors benefits the original programmer and helps to avoid large problems during testing.

The program should be coded in a language suitable for the problem programmed. This will permit easier testing. Selection of a good algorithm for solving the problem will also aid testing.

HOW MUCH TESTING

Beginning programmers always wonder how they are to know when a program has been tested enough. This is a difficult question and many a seasoned programmer has found out that he stopped testing a program too soon.

One observation is that, before testing is completed, every instruction should have been executed at least once. Test data should try every error condition possible. Each branch should be tested. Thus, on a two-way or three-way branch they would all be tried at least once. If you have some special routines to handle unusual input data, each routine should be tested at least once. Thus, all classes of input should be used as test data. While this is not a sufficient test, it is at least a necessary test. These are called *leg tests* (a test is sent through each leg in the logic of the program).

Program sections that interact heavily will have to be tested by using data that will cause the interactions to be tested thoroughly. If there are a large number of factors that influence the dependent quantities, complete testing can be difficult. Care must be taken so data are such that errors are not hidden, because they do not affect the results of a particular case.

One should avoid the temptation to drop the program as soon as it does not look incorrect. A half-tested program can prove quite embarrassing to the programmer because a half-tested program will still have to be tested later on after it has produced some embarrassing results.

Since it is seldom possible to test all possibilities of a large program, where does one stop testing? This depends on the value of the program. Considerations are:

1. Importance of accuracy.
2. How often is the program to be used?
3. How long a period will it be used?

Thus a program that is to be used once or twice would probably be tested less than a program that is to be used daily for many months. But the overriding consideration is the necessity for accuracy. In many cases, a small risk of inaccuracy is tolerable, considering the cost of trying to be certain. In reality, we are seldom certain anyway.

Number of Tests

The sheer number of tests often is of little significance itself. Programs do not wear out. That is, if a program will add some numbers correctly once it will add a group of similar numbers correctly again. Likewise, sheer quantity does not guarantee that all cases have been tested. If you process 100 records for test data from normal input data, 90 of them will be the same, that is, test the main logical sequence of the program. The last 10 will probably test only 2 additional cases. So the 100 records processed are actually only 3 different test cases.

Another reason for not using large volumes of test data is that no one is going to spend the time to examine 1,000 test cases to see if they are correct. So nothing is gained.

Too often a large number of test cases just proves the program is good at doing the same thing with different numbers. Instead, we wish to prove robustness. We want each test run to check something not checked by previous runs. The goal is to strain the program to its limit. This requires a good imagination and a suspicious nature.

SELECTING TEST DATA

The selecting of appropriate data for testing a routine can greatly ease the problem of detecting errors. The first test of the program or module should be the simplest possible. The goal is to see if the program will execute at all. This is often called a *smoke test* (plug it in and see if smoke comes out). The first few tests are used to verify the basic organization of the program, for if the basic organization is incorrect, it is frivolous as well as difficult to check out the intricacies of the program.

Thus, a test that follows the typical flow of the program will uncover gross errors. If gross errors are present, the program will easily spin off in any direction at the speed of several million operations a minute. If an elaborate test is used for the first test and the program does not work, you will not know if the program fails to work for all cases or just for this specialized case. A complicated set of test data will produce either a very simple failure that could have been found with a much simpler set of test data, or will produce a failure as complicated as the test data producing output impossible to diagnose.

Keep your arithmetic simple. If a program will add 11.11, 22.22, and 33.33 correctly, it will add 12.56, 45.92, and 34.79 correctly.

Simple test data are easier to hand check. Test cases are to see if the program works correctly, not to test the ability of the machine to perform arithmetic.

Even though it is desirable to use simple data, it is also desirable to obtain as much information as possible during each test run and to make as few runs as possible. We would like to obtain many units of information from each test run, but items being tested must not interfere with each other to the point of obscuring information in case of errors. Good tests should also help to indicate the error source if errors develop.

Some testing requires "miniaturization" of the program; that is, reducing the amount of data to a reasonable level below the regular amount of data. For example, a program may usually require a 50×50 matrix, but checking out test cases of this size is prohibitive by hand. Thus, a test matrix of 5×5 may be used. But if this requires program changes, there are some dangers that either existing errors may be obscured or temporarily eliminated by the changes, or else that new errors may be introduced in the program by the changes that are made to facilitate program testing.

Similarly, if a routine works for a loop of 5, it should work for a loop of 105 (as long as sufficient storage space is reserved). For loops, loops of size 0, 1, or a negative value (careful) often produce interesting results. If a loop is supposed to do N iterations, the most common error is to do $n - 1$ or $n + 1$ iterations.

Test data should increase in complexity stepwise. With each new test run, one new section of the program is assumed to work correctly (at least under one case). Stepwise testing makes it much easier to pinpoint an error when results are incorrect. If test data simultaneously test several untested sections of the program and the program blows up, it is very difficult to know which of the several sections caused the blow-up.

Eventually, the tests should test all sections of the program. Thus, routines with errors in them will not be skipped because they do not affect the results in that particular case.

When testing a program the goal is not just to see if the program executes for each set of test data; the goal is to see that the program executes *correctly*. Thus, test data should be chosen so the programmer can calculate the correct answer *before* the program is run. If the answer is calculated after the test run, it is too easy to assume that the answer is correct.

TYPES OF TEST DATA

There are three general categories of test data:

1. Constructed data.
2. Actual data with modifications.
3. Actual data in volume.

Each type of data is usually needed to test a program.

Constructed data is the first test data used. *Constructed* test data are the data the programmer creates (constructs) to test the program. There are two types of constructed test data: controlled and random. The controlled test data are used to see if the program works at all. Controlled test data have the advantage that they can be created to test particular situations that might rarely occur. Such creation allows the maximum control over test data. Also, selection of the right data will minimize the necessary work needed to hand-check results. The drawback with controlled test data is that only those problems that the user recognizes as problems are included in the test data.

Thus, one should not overlook using random test data. Random test data are often created by a special program provided for this purpose. Controlled test data may consistently avoid the errors in the program. Random test data have the advantage of indicating errors that may not be apparent otherwise. The disadvantage of using random test data is it may be difficult to check the results to see if they are correct. But if the errors resulting are gross enough (abnormal termination), they will be quite apparent.

Modified actual data has some of the advantages of both other types of data. By careful selective modification of real data, specific tests can be made with the program. The use of real data avoids a sometimes awesome task of keypunching large masses of data.

Another advantage of using modified real data is that it adds an element of reality to the testing process. The introduction of real data can pinpoint many problem areas that could never be discovered by constructed data. One reason for modifying real data is to test error routines. Deliberate introduction of errors in data is the only way to make sure the error-checking routines work.

The final set of test data is volume testing by using actual live data. If this can be done with a parallel run of an older system, there will be less hand checking to be done on resulting calculations. Many surprises are usually in store for the programmer when using real data. Often this is where a failure of communication between the user and programmer is discovered. Oversights by both programmer and user are often revealed here.

Occasionally, parallel runs will demonstrate that the older system had in fact been incorrect in part. Checking of expected output without a parallel run is usually a very time-consuming job, if at all possible. Parallel test runs of at least three cycles are usually necessary for complete testing.

It would seem that all three types of test data are needed to do a complete job of testing. Each type has its advantages and disadvantages if used alone; but, when used together, they tend to balance each other, thus providing the best possibility of thorough testing.

When hand-calculating results to check out test calculations, enough care should be taken to get correct results. Otherwise, you could compare your incorrect hand-calculated results and the computer printout, and spend many hours looking for a bug in the program when the problem is in your calculations.

SOLUTIONS FOR TEST DATA

If test data are to be used, one must be able to figure out if the program-generated answers are correct. There are several ways to obtain correct answers:

1. Calculate the answer by hand calculations.
2. Obtain results from a book, article, or set of tables.
3. Obtain the answer from another computer program.

It is important that the results produced by the program can be compared with corresponding data obtained *independently* from a different source. Obviously, the first method is the most undesirable since it may require a great deal of work to calculate the answers by hand.

All the above techniques require you to know what the expected output values are. Sometimes this is not possible or practical for all test data. Then there are two additional methods that are possible if the tester has detail knowledge of the program algorithm.

The first method requires knowing the magnitude of the output values. The magnitude can usually be determined by rough analysis and knowledge of the algorithm. Any output values that exceed the expected ranges can be checked out more carefully.

The second method is by manipulating the test data in a controlled manner. By carefully modifying input values, one should be able to predict direction and magnitude of change in the resulting output values. This should partially indicate whether the program is operating correctly.

GENERATING TEST DATA

In order to aid testing, there should be means to generate test data. For card data this can be as simple as providing standard test cards. Standard test cards usually include:

1. A card with   0 in columns 1–9,
                        1 in columns 10–19,
                        2 in columns 20–29,
                        etc.

2. Cards with   1 in column 1,
                        2 in column 2,
                        ·
                        ·

                        9 in column 9,
                        0 in column 10,
                        1 in column 11,
                        ·
                        ·

                        9 in column 19,
                        0 in column 20,
                        1 in column 21,
                        etc.

3. Cards with   80 columns of zeros
    Cards with   80 columns of ones
         ·
         ·

    Cards with   80 columns of nines

4. Cards that alternate zeros and ones.
5. 80 column alphabetic cards: A in column 1,
                                        B in column 2,
                                        C in column 3,
                                        etc.

This type of test data can be used to check out fields. For example, if columns 27–32 are used for input, then records with data like cards 1 and 2 can be used. Then the output would look as follows:

222333
789012   (Read each column as a number.)

The above clearly indicates the columns that were read (that is, 27, 28, ... 32). This proves one of the most basic things to be tested; that is, that the correct columns of the records are being read. Then test cards of types 3-5 can be used to insure that zeros and alphabetic data are handled correctly.

No one should expect all their testing problems to be completed by using these test cards, but there are many simple tests that can be accomplished with them. The cards should be readily available in a card rack where the programmer can reach them.

Both COBOL and PL/I make heavy use of files, so test data are needed to test files. Utility programs can usually be used to create files. IBM offers the utility program IEBDG (data generator) that provides a "pattern" of test data that can be used in testing. In addition, some installations provide special test generator programs that will generate test files. The general principle of these test generator programs is that they use the file description in the program to be tested to generate test files. A test generator program can be an in-house program or one that is purchased from a software house.

TEST CASES

The actual testing of a program can be broken into three phases:

1. Testing the normal cases.
2. Testing the extremes.
3. Testing the exceptions.

These three phases should include all necessary testing.

The goal is to ensure that all valid data yield correct results, and that all invalid data always yield error messages.

Testing Normal Cases

The normal cases include the most general data for which the program was planned. Very few programs will work for all data. Instead, the data are usually restricted to a data domain; that is, the data that the program will process correctly. This phase of testing attempts to prove that the program will produce correct results for most general sets of expected data.

Testing Extremes

This is the second phase of testing. After the normal cases have been tested the extremes should be tested. The extremes include fringes of the input range that are to be accepted as valid data. For nonnumerical data, use typical and similar cases that contain all expected characteristics. For numerical data, take values at the end of the allowable range, varying for minimum and maximum field length. Obvious examples are very large numbers, very small numbers, 1 single transaction, and zero amount transactions. Each program has its own extreme data that must be selected by the programmer.

The *null* cases are always of particular interest. The null case for numerical input is usually zero values. For character strings the null case is the blank string or null string. For pointers it is the null pointer. The null case is one of the best test cases since it will surely turn up as data sometime in the life of the program. And the null case, if untested, often causes a program to do strange things.

It isn't always obvious what values will test the extremes. For example, say a program had to read in 4 positive integer 1-digit numbers. A naive approach would be to use the following to test the extremes:

	A	B	C	D
Test group 1	0	0	0	0
Test group 2	9	9	9	9

At first glance these would seem to be the extreme values.

The above sets of numbers are good test cases, but they probably are not the desired extremes. They are the extremes only if the calculation is:

$$ANSWER = A + B + C + D$$

But if the calculation being performed is:

$$ANSWER = (\frac{A+B}{C}) ** D$$

then a value of $C = 1$ would give the largest possible answer.

$$ANSWER = (\frac{9+9}{9}) **9 = 2^9$$

$$ANSWER = (\frac{9+9}{1}) **9 = 18^9$$

Therefore, it is possible to select the numeric values that will produce the extremes only if you are familiar with the actual calculations being done. The major reason for wishing to use the extremes in test calculations is to insure that intermediate result fields have sufficient space to handle the calculation.

Test situations can be forced by loading in data as constants to create the test conditions desired. If the extreme conditions that you want to test are the result of long calculations, it may be difficult to manufacture data to create the condition you wish to test. For example, if you wish to test the condition of a calculation turning negative, a relatively rare situation, then this can easily be done by adding a statement in the program to reset the necessary variable to negative to complete the test. Care must be taken to remove this modification after testing is completed. An easy way to remember to remove it, is to insert a comment stating that it is a test statement. I always keypunch TEST in columns 73–80 of my source test card as a reminder.

Testing Exceptions

The final phase is the testing of data that falls outside the acceptable range. All programs are designed to process a restricted set of data. Thus, if the program is not designed to handle negative or zero data, what happens when it is actually given this type of erroneous input? Or, if arrays are used, what happens if the number of data elements exceed the size of the specified arrays? What happens if strings are too long or too short? What happens if numbers are too large or too small?

The worst thing that can happen is that the program accepts the erroneous data and returns an incorrect but believable answer. It is not sufficient to say that the program wasn't designed for that data, or to say no erroneous data should be inputted. Erroneous data can be inputted through keypunch errors or a misunderstanding of input instructions. The program should forcefully reject all data it cannot process correctly.

If you are going to be the sole user of the program, you may decide to live dangerously and skip adding program statements to reject bad data. But if the program is for others to use, there must be statements to reject any unacceptable data. These statements must be tested and the tests must convince you that you haven't overlooked any editing statements.

When testing the exceptions or the extremes, there are several hints that can usually save time. If there are edit checks that include range tests, try values on both sides of the range. Usually those values just inside or outside the range are the ones most likely to give trouble.

Data with blanks, numerics, and alphabetic characters should all be tried in various combinations. That is, try a blank field and an alphabetic field in fields that require numeric data. If relations between data fields are being tested, try permutations of correct and incorrect data.

Sometimes data with multiple input errors can cause unusual problems. If these problems are not discovered during testing, they will surely present themselves during production runs.

Now is the time to be curious and let your imagination run wild. Put in out-of-sequence data. Try a handful of data cards from the recycling bin. Try some data cards upside down. Try a data tape from another job. The first rule of data is: "Data will be incorrect."

If your program is not designed to prevent the using of incorrect data, you will spend a lot of time looking for bugs when the fault is the data. While it may be careless for a clerk to prepare incorrect data, it is unforgivable for the programmer to allow the program to accept the incorrect data as correct.

SAMPLE TESTS

A very simple problem to test would be a module that calculates the diagonal of a box. Figure 5.1 shows a box with a diagonal drawn. The diagonal is equal to $\sqrt{(\sqrt{A^2 + C^2})^2 + B^2}$.

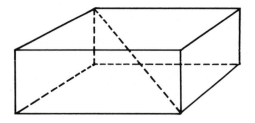

Figure 5.1

For test data we wish to test the normal cases, the extremes, and the exceptions.

	Sides of a Box			Remarks
1.	1	1	1	A good first test.
2.	1	2	3	Another normal test.
3.	0	0	0	Should give you a zero answer.
4.	0	1	2	Not a box. What happens?
5.	1	0	3	Not a box. What happens?
6.	2	1	0	Not a box. What happens?
7.	1	−6	3	Incorrect data.

The first two tests are testing the normal cases. Tests 3–7 test the extremes or exceptions. If all these tests produce correct answers, then we are fairly sure that the module works correctly. You might like to try some large or small numbers as an additional test. One is never positive that a program will always work, but in this case we would have a high degree of expectation.

A second example of testing is the finding of quadratic roots of the equation $Ax^2 + Bx + C = 0$. In this program we read the coefficients A, B, C and use the quadratic formula

$$R = \frac{b \pm \sqrt{b^2 - 4ac}}{2a}$$

to find the two roots. We have a few more things to test here.

	Coefficients			Remarks
1.	1	1	−2	A good first test.
2.	1	0	0.25	Another normal test.
3.	0	0	0	What happens here?
4.	0	2	1	Should get only 1 root.
5.	2	1	0	Should be O.K.
6.	1	1	1	Imaginary roots.
7.	0	0	2	Not a valid equation.
8.	0	2	0	Should get 1 root.
9.	2	0	0	Should get 2 roots.

If all these test data produce correct results, we would again be reasonably certain that the program would produce good results consistently.

There are two things to notice here. The first is that these were simple routines to test. If you use module programming, your routines can also be simple. The second thing to notice is that the testing was done in a systematic fashion. We did not just pick several random numbers as test data. Normally, if random numbers are used for test data, it is too difficult to calculate the results by hand. Also random numbers may not test all cases. It is better to carefully pick input that will test all the possible situations in the program. Good testing is thorough testing.

MODULES

I imagine some of the programmers reading this chapter thought the testing examples were nice, but nowhere near the complicated programs they do. Well, your programs can be simple if you use modules. Only very inexperienced programmers write single, long, untestable programs. It is virtually impossible to test a large mono-lithic program because of the large number of total logic paths. The more experienced the programmer, the more short modules he writes.

The major aim of modules is to produce readily testable units. Each module should do one task. Then, in the testing of the unit, we must test only to see if this one task is completed correctly. Modules that have been individually tested have a much better chance of producing a correct program. All modules should be completely tested before they are combined.

Once the individual modules are tested, then the paths and interactions between the modules must be tested. Even though the data areas might have been checked during debugging, it is good idea to verify that all values being passed between modules are correct since it is a very common area of trouble. Because the interaction between the modules is restricted by the parameter list, testing of a large program composed of modules is easier than a large program without modules. At this stage of testing there should be no logic errors in the individual modules. If an error is discovered, it would indicate that module testing was incomplete.

The chance of introducing errors when program changes are made is substantially reduced when small modules are used. Modules can also be easily included in a library. Then the use of the library programs automatically reduces the testing job since the routines contained in the library are pretested.

Simulation of Modules

A common situation is the need to simulate a module. Possibly a needed module is not ready but is needed to complete testing of another module. In order to start testing the completed module, the missing module can be simulated. There are two possibilities: dummy modules or substitution modules.

Dummy Modules. A dummy module is one that has only an entry point and a return point. It is used to test a higher-level module when the needed module is not ready or not required. It is often useful to have a statement in the dummy module that will indicate it was called.

Substitution Modules. A substitution module is used for testing when a dummy module cannot be used. The substitution module actually does some calculation, but usually only in a very simplified manner. It is needed because a higher module calls the substitution module to return some values so testing of the upper module can be completed.

Another reason to use a substitution module is that the needed module may require too much computer time or special output to use the real module, so it is advantageous to use a substitution module to speed up testing.

Hints on Testing Modules

Testing of modules can be made easier by placing the data in the top module. This results in easier testing because then all data is external to the lower modules being tested. For example, maybe the I/O module requires a fairly complicated coding that will take a long time to program. Many of the other modules may be programmed earlier. To avoid delay in testing the other modules, a substitution I/O module could be set up to provide test input data. Since all the data are kept in the top module it would be fairly simple to program a substitution module to provide test input data. Then the other modules can proceed in testing without having to wait for the I/O module.

Each module should be short in length and thus easily comprehended. Each module should have a limited number of paths and process a small amount of data. If the module has all the above conditions, it should be relatively simple to test the module, using all the extremes of the data, and to test each process path.

Another method to test modules is to use an "initial" statement in the module to start testing. The initial statement can provide the first values to test the module. This method avoids the problem of actually having to pass values to the module. This provides a good way to first test the module. But you will still have to test the module and pass values to it since there can be errors in the passing of values that would be overlooked by the initializing test method.

EARLY TESTING

Modules offer a chance to begin testing early. If an error is found when the program specification is being drawn up, it is easy to fix it.

If the error is found when testing a small segment or a low-level module, it is not very difficult to fix. But if an error is found when the whole program is being tested, it will involve several people, communication between groups, and resulting delay and confusion.

Finally, errors in production programs involve the original programmers, hold up processing, and cause rerunning of the job. Usually a temporary fix is needed and maybe communication is needed between the program developer at a remote location and the user location. Thus, it is important that testing begins as soon as possible. A basic rule is: "The earlier an error is discovered, the less it will cost to fix."

PROGRAM LIBRARY

As the subroutines are coded, debugged and tested, they should be put in a library. This will reduce the size of test decks and, more important, ensure that all programs requiring a particular routine are actually using the same version.

Sometimes it is desirable to have two program libraries: one a test library and the other a production library. The test library can contain subroutines with test aids (or debug aids) built in. By using the statement

IF TESTING THEN ...

described in the debugging chapter, one can usually get the same result with only one program library.

FILE TESTING

When processing records where the record changes, the record should be printed out before and after each change. Similarly, when the response to a record depends on what is in the record, the record should be printed. This will facilitate testing since it allows the tester to avoid reading dumps of files.

A set of test records should be created early in the testing process to reduce duplication of effort. Utility programs are usually available for convenient generating of test records. A record generator program can greatly facilitate testing of programs. The program should be able to generate records for testing when data formats, including size, character, and normal contents of each field, are given it.

SYSTEM TESTING

So far this chapter has been devoted to program testing. But there is often the bigger test situation, that is, system testing. The system may include several programs and in between clerical tasks.

System testing proceeds from the simple to the complex. The testing of large systems is usually divided up into the following steps:

Unit Testing. The *unit test* is the lowest level of testing. The innermost routines are tested first. Testing should include all possible valid inputs and a sufficiently large collection of erroneous input to test all error routines.

Module Testing. The module can be a single program of a system or a system routine. The programmer should test his own modules before releasing them to the next step.

System Testing. The modules are put together and tested as a group. Major errors in coordinating the system are discovered here. The tests should be prepared by the person who prepared the program specifications.

Product Testing. Here the complete package is checked out, including documentation.

Field Testing. This is often called validation. The system is released to a restricted group of users. The system is closely watched for errors. Documentation shortcomings can be corrected here. This restricted group of users should be encouraged to run test cases of their own and to attempt to "crash" the system.

Release Testing. The product is released for general use. The user always completes the final testing. Now it is found out how thoroughly the previous testing has been done.

There are several helpful observations that can be made about organized testing patterns as the above.

1. Take only one step at a time, holding as many environmental factors constant as possible.
2. In the actual tests, proceed from the simple to the complex. The volume of test entries and the complexity of test entries should increase gradually.
3. If a program chronically fails at a given level of testing, it should be demoted to the previous level for additional testing.
4. An analogous rule is that the amount of difficulty encountered at any step of testing varies inversely with the thoroughness of the preceding steps of testing.
5. Loose control over the coding and debugging only delays the ultimate problems until testing.
6. Careless program testing reveals itself during "production" runs.

USE YOUR PROGRAM TO CHECK OUTPUT

A program can be used to help check out the answers. For example, if a module was to find a square root, the best approach would be for the test routine to call the square root module, then print out the returned square root, the square of this supposed root, and the difference between the input argument and the square of the returned root. There are many other cases where the program can be used to check the answers.

But one must be careful not to let the program convince you that an incorrect answer is correct. If you have the computer print out the intermediate calculations and then verify each step, all you have done is verify that the machine can multiply correctly. You have not verified that it did the correct mathematical operations in the correct order. In the square root example, calculations were done in two different ways and the results compared. This is not foolproof, but it is still a good check.

VALIDATION

At some point testing is considered completed. The program has been tested thoroughly with test and real data. The data preparation and operating instructions are reviewed and considered complete. If possible, release the program to a restricted number of users. A restricted release provides an additional testing phase before the program is completely released.

All final testing is always done by the user. Computer manufacturer's software is always tested by the user. Very seldom can the programmer have foreseen and tested all possible areas of difficulties. Users will normally report any errors they find which can be corrected and the program retested. Then the test data previously developed can be used to retest after changes.

Once the program has passed this limited usage test, it is ready for final release. All input instructions and documentation should be completely updated.

ADEQUATE TIME FOR TESTING

One way to help guarantee adequate testing is to schedule sufficient time for it. One suggested amount of time necessary for testing is that the testing will probably take at least as long as the programming took. Debugging usually takes at least three or four times as long as writing the program. Since the tendency is to schedule only time for programming, this might indicate why all programming projects are late. Time should be scheduled for planning, coding, debugging, and testing. Then, if the planning is two weeks behind schedule, it is obvious that everything else will also be two weeks behind schedule.

On systems where thorough testing is required, extra time is needed. On the Apollo program, according to estimates by NASA, testing accounted for 80% of the cost of developing software. This is a high figure because of the thoroughness required in Apollo testing, but similar estimates for the development of operational software have produced figures of 30% to 60% of the total development cost as the amount assigned to testing.

Testing Schedules

If program testing is divided into categories, it is much easier to control testing. Very often a set amount of time is scheduled for all testing. Thus, trouble in one area will steal testing time from other areas.

Instead, a set amount of time should be scheduled for each step of testing. Then, if unit testing is two weeks behind schedule, management will be warned early that the job production schedule will be delayed two weeks if additional resources are not allocated. Often, in order to keep on schedule when delays have occurred, later steps of testing are just skipped.

Testing schedules allow tighter control over testing and early warning if testing is not going according to schedule.

A Program Test Schedule

Quite often it is desirable to keep track of how program testing is progressing. At least two things are of interest:

Are we maintaining our schedule?
Is the program being properly tested?

Both questions are very important and very difficult to answer. But there are techniques that can help to indicate the status of program testing.

Large program systems are usually divided into subsystems or components. These components are then composed of the smallest identifiable program units. There may be many levels and many units at each level.

The normal method of testing is to test the smallest unit first, then combine the units and continue testing the combined units until the complete system is tested.

An approach to organized testing is to develop a library of test cases while the program is being coded. This should be a parallel development effort by a different group from the programming group.

This assumes that the test group and program group both use the same program specifications. If the specifications are not clear, then the tests designed usually will not match the programs. These tests thus help prove the clearness of the design specifications. Separate design of test cases verifies both program testing and specification testing. If the program will not run with the supplied tests, this may indicate a specification failure rather than a test failure or program failure.

Once the test cases are designed by the test group, a status report can be kept of the following rates of progress:

What percent of tests have been tried?
What percent of tests have been completed successfully?

By keeping daily records of test results, management should be able to have some indication of program testing progress.

If an effort is not made to develop systematic test cases, then it is doubtful if any true indication of status or success of testing can be found. Too many programming systems have failed from lack of any careful long-range test planning and from lack of understanding the intensive and exhausive effort necessary for comprehensive system testing.

HOW WELL HAS A PROGRAM BEEN TESTED?

Sometimes on a program it is desirable to know how well the code has been tested. If the program is large with many logical decisions, then a pessimistic evaluation would be that most programs have not been very well tested. But it still would be useful to have a yardstick to determine how well the program has been tested. Some of the things to use in an evaluation are:

1. The percent of code actually executed during tests. We should hope for 100% here.
2. The percent of the total number of branches that has been taken in both directions during testing. Again we would try to obtain 100% here.
3. How well has the program been segmented? Segmented programs are usually easier to test, and thus are better tested.
4. The extent to which various interlock situations had been explored.

The weakest part of the testing is usually the last one.

On a large program it would be impossible to test all logical paths and data dependencies, but all the major paths should be covered. Then the programmer is required to use his intuition to decide which untested paths would be most productive to test (that is, the paths most prone to error). At this stage, program testing is no longer a science but becomes an art. Since the combinations and permutations of logical paths may be astronomical, a large program can never be completely tested. But there are two paths of special interest: the path of minimum input and the path of maximum input. These paths are usually easily identifiable and should be tested. Some of the considerations the program tester must consider are the importance of the logical paths, the prior testing completed, the vulnerability to failure, the cost of testing, and possible payoff.

RETESTING

During testing it is common to have to make changes in the program because of errors found while testing. These changes are particularly vulnerable to producing new errors. This is because your mind is committed to removing the present error, and it is easy to overlook other problems that may be introduced. Program modification is also quite vulnerable to introducing errors. If previous test data have been saved, the old test data can be used to make sure new errors have not been introduced.

A file should be kept of old test data. The test data can be stored on a magnetic tape or in any other convenient form. Then the test tape can be periodically rerun. Previous test output should have been saved. If previous test output is not saved, the results will have to be recalculated. If previous test output is saved, one just compares new and old output.

If test output is voluminous, then it should be put on a tape. A utility program can be used to compare the new and old, printing out any differences. If there is voluminous test output, sight comparison is inadequate and unpractical.

Retesting is sometimes called *redundancy testing* or *regression testing*. When programs are first tested we start with small, simple test cases and proceed to the large, complex tests. In regression testing we can start testing with the large, complex test and proceed to the small, simple test cases only if the large, complex tests are unsuccessful. As we proceed backwards to the simpler tests, the errors should be localized.

A TEST GROUP

One approach that has been tried is to establish a group of senior programmers to test all programs and systems before they are actually used for production runs. This does not free the original programmer from testing his program. The testing group provides a final test for programs after the original programmer has certified the program as correct.

The test group can then consider the program a "black box" where, if specified input is provided, the outcome will be the desired results. Test groups are sometimes called professional idiots (not meant as an insult).

These are people who are good at designing incorrect data. That is, they design data that an idiot (hence, the name) would use as input. The professional tester's job is to be destructive. His goal is to attempt to cause the system to fail. If he makes the system fail, he is successful. The original programmer wants to make the program succeed. Thus, the original programmer and tester have different goals.

A test group can thus gain proficiency in testing. Also, a fresh mind often can see problems that the original programmer may have overlooked. Thus, sometimes it is advisable to have a friend test your program.

Testing done by a test group is sometimes called *acceptance testing*. The original programmers test the programs deductively and analytically, using their superior knowledge of the inner logic of the program. But the acceptance-tester approach is basically empirical since he knows little of the internal logic of the program. The acceptance tester can be considered a middle man between the program developer and the eventual user.

The acceptance tester must rely on the program specifications. If the specifications are vague or inconsistent, he will discover this when he tries to test the program. The acceptance tester must decide if the program accomplishes the purpose set out in the original program specifications. If the program test group cannot determine from the specifications what the program is supposed to do, no testing can be accomplished.

Also, the acceptance tester may determine things like:

Are the results accurate enough?

Is the documentation complete enough to allow easy use of the program?

Are error situations taken care of sufficiently?

Some of the advantages of using a testing group are:

1. The testing group does not disband at the end of each project. Thus, it can accumulate testing experience and develop special tools to make testing more thorough and efficient.
2. The testing group's loyalty is directed to the user, and not against his colleagues who developed the programs. The test group's job is not to prove the developer did his work correctly. Instead, it is to prove that the program is acceptable to the ultimate user.
3. Since the testing group is working for the user, they can influence the program developer to do adequate testing.

CONCLUSION

A programmer is judged by the number of errors that arise after the program is released for general use. Thus, it is better to have a reputation of being slow but producing good and thoroughly checked-out programs, than to have a reputation of being fast but producing error-prone programs. The production of error-free programs is a time-consuming task.

A common piece of programming graffiti is: "Why do we never have enough time to do it right the first time, but always have plenty of time to fix it later?" Quick and dirty programmers tend to tarnish the reputation of all programmers since these programs too are expected to turn out correct results. All important programs are always assigned to the programmer who turns out good, thoroughly checked-out code. Since your programming reputation is involved, it is wise to insist that enough time be allowed for proper program testing. Inadequate time produces inadequate results. But adequate time better produces adequate results.

EXERCISES

1. Take a program you are familiar with and design test cases for:
   (a) The normal cases.
   (b) The extreme cases.
   (c) The exceptional cases.

2. What are some of the advantages to using subroutines when testing?

3. Write a program to find the cube root and use your program to check the accuracy.

4. What excuses are used for a program when it fails?

5. Think of a program that failed during a production run. Would a well-planned testing practice have uncovered the error?

6. How does program debugging differ from program testing? Do you believe program testing should be a separate step from program debugging? Why?

7. Define:
   Program robustness.
   Specifications testing.
   Leg test.
   Smoke test.
   Unit test.
   System test.
   Product testing.
   Field testing.
   Release testing.
   Validation.
   Redundancy testing.
   Professional idiot.

8. Devise a method to evaluate how well a program is tested. For example, 100% tested means you guarantee no errors will result.

9. When is the artisan program tester needed?

10. Take a program and prepare the following test data:
    (a) Constructed data.
    (b) Actual data with modifications.
    (c) Actual data in volume.

11. Name three ways of obtaining results for test data.

12. What automatic testing routines are available for your programming language?

13. What utility programs are available for program testing?

14. What are some of the advantages to setting up a testing schedule?

15. Using your own programming experience, figure out what percent of your time is used for coding, debugging, and testing.

16. Why is retesting important?

17. Given the following formula:

$$Y = \frac{ab}{cd} - \frac{c+d}{a-b}$$

prepare test cases for
(a) The normal cases.
(b) The extreme cases.
(c) The exceptional cases.

18. Write a program to find roots of quadratic equations:

$$ax^2 + bx + c = 0$$

Use the formula:

$$\text{Roots} = \frac{-b \pm \sqrt{b^2 - 4ac}}{2a}$$

Use the program to check out the roots you find. That is, substitute the calculated roots into the input equation to see if the result is zero. Test the program by using your own test data.

Next, use the following test data.

a	b	c	a	b	c
1	2	1	6	5	-4
1	-1	-6	$6*10^{30}$	$5*10^{30}$	$-4*10^{30}$
1	-10	1	10^{-30}	-10^{30}	10^{30}
1	-1000	1	1.0	-4.0	3.9999999
1	-10000	1	1.0	-4.0	4.0
1	2	3	1.0	100.0001	0.01

Finally, reprogram the problem by using extended precision, and see if the results improve.

19. Develop test data for the following program: Your teacher, Ironsides Gradehard, believes in "survival of the fittest." Here is the grading algorithm. Calculate the mean (u) and standard deviation (s) of the class scores. Let t_i be the test scores. Then

$$ u = \sum_{i=1}^{n} \frac{t_i}{n} $$

$$ s = \left(\sum_{i=1}^{n} \frac{(t_i - u)^2}{n} \right)^{1/2} $$

Grades are assigned according to the following rules:
"A" for scores greater than or equal to $u + 2s$.
"B" for scores greater than or equal to $u + s$, but less than $u + 2s$.
"C" for scores greater than or equal to $u - s$, but less than $u + s$.
"D" for scores greater than or equal to $u - 2s$, but less than $u - s$.
"F" for scores less than $u - 2s$.

20. Your computer handles a maximum of 6 significant digits. But you had to do addition with 8 significant digits. You have decided to solve this problem by splitting the input values into the left and right 4 digits and doing the addition. For example, the number 00123456 would be input as 0012 and 3456.

00123456		0012	3456
65432100	becomes	6543	2100
		6555	5556

Your program must accept both positive and negative numbers. Develop the test data for this problem first. Then program and test it, using your test data.

21. Develop some test data for the following program. Write a seat-reservation system for an airplane company. There are five

flights daily. The flight numbers are 142, 148, 153, 181, and 191. Your company takes reservations only one week in advance. Your program must accept reservations, cancellations, and refuse reservations when a flight is full. In order to reduce test input, use a plane capacity of six passengers. There are three classes of seats: first, coach, and student. The program can be made more complicated by allowing first-class passengers to bump coach passengers, and coach passengers to bump student passengers, etc.

22. Here are several methods of evaluating software reliability:
    (a) *Mean time between errors (MTBE).* The average up-times between interruptions to service.
    (b) *Mean time to repair (MTTR).* After an error is found, how long does it require to get it properly corrected?
    (c) *Percent up-time.* What percent of the time is the software operational?
    (d) *Number of bugs vs. calendar months.* Plot the number of bugs vs. calendar months and use the slope of the curve as a rough measure of progress.
    Discuss or try some of these methods for evaluating reliability of your software.

REFERENCES

Boehm, Barry W. "Some Information Processing Implications of Air Force Space Missions in the 1970's," *Astronautics and Aeronautics.* January, 1971.

Elmendorf, William R. "Controlling the Functional Testing of an Operating System," *IEEE Transactions on Systems Science and Cybernetics.* October, 1969.

Ginzberg, M. G. "Notes on Testing Real-Time System Programs," *IBM Systems Journal.* Vol 4, No. 1. 1965.

Gruenberger, Fred. "Program Testing and Validating," *Datamation.* July, 1968.

Harrison, William L. "Program Testing," *Data Management.* December, 1969.

Head, Robert V. "Testing Real-Time Systems, Part I: Development and Management," *Datamation.* July, 1964.

Head, Robert V. "Testing Real-Time Systems, Part II: Levels of Testing," *Datamation.* August, 1964.

Henry, R. W. *IAT Programming Standards and Procedures.* The Institute for Advanced Technology. Control Data Corporation. 1971.

Hetzel, William C., Editor. *Program Test Methods.* Englewood Cliffs, N.J.: Prentice-Hall, Inc. 1973.

Judd, D. R. "Program Testing and Validation," *The Computer Bulletin.* March, 1967.

Karush, Arnold D. "Program Quality Assurance," *Datamation.* October, 1968.

Leeds, Herbert D., and Gerald M. Weinberg. *Computer Programming Fundamentals.* New York: McGraw-Hill Book Company, Inc. 1966.

Management Planning Guide for a Manual of Data Processing Standards. C20-1670. IBM Corporation.

Maynard, Jeff. *Modular Programming.* Philadelphia, Pa.: Auerbach Publishers, Inc. 1972.

Maynard, Jeff. "Objective of Program Design," *Software Age.* August/September, 1970.

Noot, Dr. Vander. "System Testing," *Datamation.* November 15, 1971.

Pietrasanta, A. M. "Management Control in Program Testing." Technical Report. TR 00.1474. July 25, 1966. IBM Systems Development Division, Poughkeepsie Laboratory, New York.

Rustin, Randall, Editor. *Debugging Techniques in Large Systems,* Englewood Cliffs, N.J.: Prentice-Hall, Inc. 1971.

If a program is worth writing, it is worth writing correctly.
If you haven't made mistakes, you will get the right answer.

Program in haste, debug at your leisure.

VI

101 Programming Problems

NUMBER PROBLEMS

1. An automorphic number is one that appears at the end of its square, that is:

$$5^2 = 25$$
$$25^2 = 625$$

Write a program to find some automorphic numbers.

2. Write all of the prime numbers between 100 and 300. A prime number N is divisible only by 1 and N.

3. Every integer number can be factored in a unique way into powers of prime numbers. Write a program to do this.

4. The Goldbach conjecture is that every even number can be represented as the sum of two prime numbers. Check his conjecture for the first 500 even numbers.

5. Write a program to read two integer numbers and determine if they are relatively prime. Two numbers are relatively prime if they have no common divisors.

6. *Twin Primes.* Twin primes are two numbers which are primes and have a difference of two, that is:

$$\begin{array}{cc} 3 & 5 \\ 11 & 13 \end{array}$$

Find fifteen twin primes.

7. *Mersenne Primes.* A Mersenne prime is a prime number of the form

$$2^p - 1$$

   where p itself is prime. Write a program to find some of these numbers.

8. Pythagorean numbers can be described as follows:

$$a^2 + b^2 = c^2$$

   where a, b, c are integers. Write a program to find 5 values for c which are Pythagorean numbers. For example:

$$3^2 + 4^2 = 5^2$$

9. A perfect number is an integer that is equal to the sum of all its factors except itself. Write a program to find 3 perfect numbers. For example:

$$28 = 1 + 2 + 4 + 7 + 14$$

10. Write a program that reads a real number and prints the number in scientific notation. For example:

$$123.42 \rightarrow .12342E+03$$

11. *Fibonacci Numbers.* Here are the rules for Fibonacci numbers:

$$F_1 = 1$$
$$F_2 = 1$$
$$F_{i+2} = F_{i+1} + F_i \qquad i \geqslant 1$$

   Thus, $F_3 = 2$, $F_4 = 3$. Print the first 15 Fibonacci numbers.

12. Write a program to read in a decimal number and print its binary, octal, and hexadecimal equivalent.

13. Compute the correct arithmetic sum and difference of two integer numbers 100 digits long.

14. Write a program that will read two binary numbers and do binary addition. If you feel brave, try binary division.

15. Write a program to read N, M, and calculate N/M to 25-place accuracy.

16. Write a program to read two integer numbers and find the greatest common divisor (that is, the largest integer that will divide both input integers). The least common multiple of two integers is the product of the two numbers divided by their greatest common divisor. Find the least common divisor, too.

17. Amicable numbers are two numbers, each of which is equal to the sum of all the exact divisors of the other except that number itself. For example, 220 and 284 are amicable numbers, since 220 has the exact divisors 1, 2, 4, 5, 10, 11, 20, 22, 44, 55, and 110, whose sum is 284, and 284 has the exact divisors 1, 2, 71, 142, whose sum is 220. Write a program to find some more amicable numbers.

18. Write a program to find all the proper divisors of an integer number N (that is, all numbers less than N that divide N).

19. (a) Write a program to find the smallest integer that can be written as the sum of two cubes in two different ways. For example, the cubes are 1^3, 2^3, 3^3, ... So $9 = 1^3 + 2^3$, but it is not the sum of any other pair of cubes.

    (b) Generalize the above problem. That is, find the smallest integer M such that it is the sum of two nth powers in at least two different ways. For example:

$$\text{For } n = 1 \quad M = 2 = 0^1 + 2^1 = 1^1 + 1^1$$
$$\text{For } n = 2 \quad M = 25 = 0^2 + 5^2 = 3^2 + 4^2$$
$$\text{For } n = 3 \quad M = ? = I^3 + J^3 = K^3 + L^3$$
$$\text{For } n = 4 \quad \ldots$$
$$\vdots$$

20. Write some programs that cause arithmetic overflows for:
    (a) integer arithmetic.
    (b) real arithmetic.
    One approach is to calculate powers of 2. A faster way to get an overflow is to calculate factorials (that is, 5 factorial is

5! = 5*4*3*2*1). Also, write a program to get real arithmetic underflow.

21. Using integer values for I, J, K, L, find some numbers such that:

$$(I^3 - J^3) = (K^2 + L^2)^2$$

GAME PROBLEMS

22. Here are some games that are easily programmed.
   (a) Tic-Tac-Toe
   (b) Blackjack
   (c) Tower of Hanoi
   (d) Guess a word, by guessing one letter at a time until the word is guessed.
   (e) Nim
   (f) Craps
   (g) Slot machines
   (h) Roulette
   (i) Chinese Fan Tan
   A game can be programmed so an individual plays against the machine. Another interesting approach is to have the machine play both sides. One strategy is to program one side to play a sophisticated game, and then have the other side use a different playing strategy or have it make random moves. By printing the moves you can often watch an interesting game.

23. A bucket contains 10 black balls and 5 red balls. You draw a ball and then put it back. Then you add a ball of the same color to the bucket. Write a program to simulate 100 drawings of balls from the bucket.

24. *Missionaries and Cannibals.* Three missionaries, three cannibals, and a boat are on one side of a river. The boat will hold a maximum of two people. If the cannibals ever outnumber the missionaries on either side of the river, the cannibals will eat those missionaries. Write a program that computes how to get all the missionaries and cannibals across the river without the missionaries being eaten.

25. *Chess Fans.* Given an 8 × 8 chess board and eight queens that are hostile to each other. Find a position for each queen such that no queen may be taken by any other queen; that is, such that every row, column, and diagonal contains at most one queen.

26. *Chess Fans.* What is the maximum number of knights that can be placed on a chess board so no knight could capture another knight? This program will teach you the fact that it is important to think about the problem before programming.

27. *Chess Fans.* This is called the knight's tour. Write a program to have the knight visit each of the 64 squares without landing on any square more than once.

28. Read in student name, address, class, and major. You are the school president and must send each student a "personalized" computer letter. You must use his name, class, and major in the content of the letter. Compose a letter welcoming the student back to school, and write a program to generate these letters.

29. *Random Numbers.* A simple check for randomness is to total the number of times each digit appears in a string of random numbers. That is, you would expect 0's to appear 10% of the time, 1's to appear 10% of the time, etc. Write a program to read 100 random digits and print the percentage for each digit.

30. Write a simple mate-matching program.

31. Write a program that simulates rolling a pair of dice 1,000 times. Keep count of the number of combinations of each possible outcome. Compare your results to the theoretical outcome by calculation.

32. Write a program to calculate the odds on possible poker hands.

33. Write a program to deal cards. Then deal 1,000 poker hands and accumulate statistics on how many pairs, three of a kind, four of a kind, etc., appear. Compare your computer-generated results to a table of poker hands.

34. *Bridge Fans.* Write a program that deals a hand of bridge and then makes an opening bid.

35. *The Game of Life.* In *Scientific American*, February, 1971, the following simulation is described:

At time t a square is alive if either

(1) it was blank at time $t - 1$ and exactly 3 of its neighbors were alive;

OR

(2) it was alive at time $t - 1$ and either 2 or 3 of its neighbors were alive;

otherwise the square is blank.

A neighborhood is the eight squares touching any internal square:

X	X	X
X	Y	X
X	X	X

The 8 Xs are Ys neighbors.

This is an archetypal checkerboard simulation. It is important to calculate the configuration for each cycle as efficiently as possible. Your job will be to simulate a 15 × 15 configuration with the following squares initially alive:

(3,8), (4,7) (5,7), (5,8), (5,9), (10,7), (10,8), (10,9), (11,7), (12,8), (3,2), (4,3), (5,1), (5,2), (5,3), (9,1), (9,2), (9,3), (10,3), (11,2).

Write a program to simulate 5 cycles.

36. *Ringworm Problem.* Simulate the infection of ringworm by using an 11 × 11 array of skin cells. Start with the center cell infected. Each time unit, an infected cell has 0.5 probability of infecting each of its healthy neighbors. After 6 time units an infected cell becomes immune for 4 time units and then becomes healthy again. Simulate this infection, and print out the array for each time unit, showing which cells are infected, immune, or healthy.

GRAPHIC PROBLEMS

37. *Graphics.* Use the line printer to draw the following pictures:
(a) Print a large box.

(b)   Print a triangle.

(c)   Print a checker board of one-inch squares.   Shade the squares.

(d)   Print your name two inches high.

(e)   Plot a simple curve.

(f)   Read a radius and print a circle.

(g)   Use overprinting to develop a shading chart.   Then try to print a simple picture.

38.   Use the figure given here.

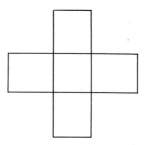

Write a program that prints all the arrangements of the digits 1-8 in the figure with the condition that no two consecutive digits can be in any adjacent squares.

39.   *Chess Players.*   The queen can move vertically, horizontally, or diagonally as far as desired.   Write a program to read the row and column of the queen as input, and mark the square the queen is on with a Q.   Mark the squares the queen could move to with *'s, and mark all other squares with +'s.   For example, a chessboard with a queen in the second row and third column would look as follows:

```
+ * * * + + + +
* * Q * * * * *
+ * * * + + + +
* + * + * + + +
+ + * + + * + +
+ + * + + + * +
+ + * + + + + *
+ + * + + + + +
```

CRYPTOGRAPHY PROBLEMS

40. Being an amateur cryptographer, you want to read alphabetic data and count the number of times each character appears. Write a program that prints frequency counts for each of the 26 letters of the alphabet and spaces. The most common letters of the English language in order of importance are ETOANIRSH. Compare this to your results.

41. Computers are an ideal tool for encoding and decoding secret messages. Write programs to do this by using the following method

    (a) *Caesar Substitution.*
        Substitute C for A.
        Substitute D for B.
        Substitute E for C, etc.

    (b) *Rail Fence Transposition.* This is a rearrangement method. Select the 1st, 4th, 7th, ... characters and place them together, followed by the 2nd, 5th, 8th, ... characters, followed by the 3rd, 6th, 9th, ... characters.

    (c) *Gronsfeld Method.* This method uses a numerical key and modifies the traditional Caesar system. Using a key 31206 and the plain text record PROGRAMMING, the following encipherment is obtained:

key	31206	31206	3
plain	PROGR	AMMIN	G
cipher	SSQGX	DNOIT	J

    To encipher P using the key digit 3, simply begin at P and count forward 3 in the normal alphabet; the substitute is S. To encipher R with key 1, begin at R and count forward 1 in the normal alphabet; the substitute is S. For decipherment, count backward in the alphabet. Two factors are evident: there are 10 possible substitutions here (for the digits 0-9) and we lose some of the weakness of the previous systems.

    (d) *Transliteration.* Another common method is to use rectangles to scramble the message. We can inscribe the alphabet into a rectangle by using a vertical path as follows:

```
1    A E I  M Q U  Y
2    B F J  N R V  Z
3    C G K O S  W
4    D H L P T  X
```

The inscription consists of taking the elements off horizontally. We will do the rows in this order 2 4 3 1. The coded message would appear as follows:

BFJNR VZDHL PTXCG KOSWA EIMQU Y

The key is the size of the rectangle and the interchanging of rows. Write a program to encode and decode messages by using this method.

CHARACTER STRING PROBLEMS

42. Read an alphabetic character string and print out the characters in reversed order.

43. Read a 5-character alphabetic character string and print all permutations of the characters.

44. Student names are punched on cards so that the last name is first, followed by a comma, then the first name and middle initial. Write a program that reads these cards and prints the names in sequence—first name, middle initial, and last name.

45. Write a subroutine that accepts character string, a single character, and then returns a number indicating how many times the single character occurs in the character string. Modify the subroutine so it searches for a substring instead of a single character.

46. Write a program that reads in a sequence of numbers. Print the longest subsequence of monotonic increasing magnitude.

47. *Roman Numbers.* Write a program to add Roman numbers. Write a program to multiply Roman numbers. Here are some Roman numbers and their decimal equivalents:

Roman	Decimal
I	1
II	2
III	3
IV	4
V	5
VI	6
.	
.	
.	
IX	9
X	10
L	50
C	100
D	500
M	1,000

Restrict the input Roman numbers to MMM (3,000).

STATISTICS PROBLEMS

48. Read in N, then read N numbers. Print the mean, standard deviation, maximum value, minimum value, and range.

49. Write a program to compute statistics of customers. Data cards will look as follows:

Field	Columns
Customer number	1–4
Age (in years)	6–7
Sex (0 female, 1 male)	9
Marital status (0 single, 1 married, 2 divorced or separated	11

Print out this information:
(a) Percent under 21 years old.
(b) Percent 21 or over.
(c) Percent male, female.
(d) Percent single.
(e) Percent married.
(f) Percent divorced or separated.
Label all output.

50. A group of students took an exam where possible scores range from 0 to 100. Write a program to print a bar graph showing the number of students that fell in the intervals 0 to 10, 11 to 20, etc.

51. Write a program to read in an array of student names and test scores. There are 15 students, and 5 test scores for each student. Compute the average for each test. Then compute the average score for each student. Then compute the student average, using the best four test scores. Finally, print the names of the students who received an average test score higher than the average, using the four-test average.

COMPILER PROBLEMS

52. Write a program for a compiler that will read cards with arithmetic expressions and check for unmatched parentheses.

53. Write a program for a compiler that will read arithmetic expressions and determine if each is a valid expression. Assume all variable names are only one character long. The following are three invalid arithmetic expressions:

$$A = B/*C$$
$$D = E * (A - B$$
$$F = G + 5 +$$

54. Write a program that reads an arithmetic statement and then does the arithmetic in the correct order. Operations are restricted to

$$( ) = - + * /$$

For example:

$$A = 5 * 3 - 4 / 2$$

In the above, the * is done first, then the /, and, finally, the subtraction.

SORTING PROBLEMS

55. Read in 3 numbers in any order. Put the numbers in order and print the ordered numbers. Next, modify the program to read N, then read N numbers, sort the numbers, and print the numbers in ascending order.

56. Write programs to do sorts by using these techniques:
    (a) *Bubble Sort.* Place the smallest element in $A(1)$. Put the second smallest element in $A(2)$. Put the third smallest element in $A(3)$, etc.
    (b) *Merge Sort.* You will need four arrays: A, B, C, D. Start with all elements in array A. Start with a_1 and put a_i in C until $a_i > a_{i+1}$. As soon as $a_i > a_{i+1}$, put a_{i+1} into array D and continue to put elements in array D until $a_i > a_{i+1}$, then switch back to array C. When array A has been exhausted you will have a series of sorted subsequences in arrays C and D. Next, take the first subsequence of arrays C and D and merge them together in sequence, placing them in array A. Next, take the second subsequence in array C and D and merge them together, placing them in array B. Then take the third subsequence in array C and D and merge them together, placing them in array A. Continue merging until arrays C and D are exhausted. Then arrays A and B are merged in a similar manner. This process is continued until one array contains all the numbers in sequence.
    (c) *Radix Sort.* Starting with the least significant column, order the numbers so the least significant column is in order. Proceed to the higher-order columns, ordering them one at a time, taking care not to scramble the order of the less significant columns. To make it easier, use only positive integer numbers. If you wish to make it more difficult, drop this last restriction. A card sorter uses a radix sort.
    (d) Develop another method of sorting and program it.
    (e) Compare the different methods of sorting to see which is faster. One method of comparing the time used is to generate 1,000 random numbers, sort them, and see which sorting method is the fastest.

MATHEMATICS PROBLEMS

57. Write a program to read in three numbers.
    (a) Determine if it cannot be a triangle.
    (b) Determine if it is an equilateral triangle.
    (c) Determine if it is an isosceles triangle.
    (d) Determine if it is a right triangle.

58. Write a program to read in 4 numbers. Can these form a quadrangle? Square? Rectangle? Parallelogram? Rhombus?

59. Write a program to read the coefficients of three linear equations and find the solutions for the three unknowns.

60. The famous computer scientist, Professor Abort Easycode, is engaged in testing his new computer by trying the $81*10^9$ possible solutions to the problem of reconstructing the following exact long division in which all the digits, except one in the quotient, have been replaced by a star:

$$
\begin{array}{r}
8 \\
*** \overline{)\,********} \\
*** \\
\hline
**** \\
*** \\
\hline
**** \\
****
\end{array}
$$

    (a) Each * denotes a digit between 0 and 9 and all leading digits are nonzero. Find a solution to the above.
    (b) How many actual solutions are there?

61. Write programs to compute 20 terms of the following:
    (a) $\pi = 4(1 - 1/3 + 1/5 - 1/7 + \ldots)$
    (b) $e = 1 + 1/1 + 1/2! + 1/3! + 1/4! + \ldots$
    (c) $\sinh x = x^1/1! + x^3/3! + x^5/5! + \ldots$
    (d) $e^x = 1 + x/1! + x^2/2! + x^3/3! + x^4/4! + \ldots$
    (e) $\sin^{-1} x = x + 1/2 \cdot x^3/3 + 1/2 \cdot 3/4 \cdot x^5/5 + 1/2 \cdot 3/4 \cdot 5/6 \cdot x^7/7 + \ldots$

62. Write four subroutines to perform complex arithmetic, one for each of addition, subtraction, multiplication, and division.

63. Write programs that will add, subtract, and multiply polynomials. Use vectors to store the coefficients of each polynomial.

64. *Newton-Raphson Method.* The square root of A can be found by using this iterative formula.

$$x_{i+1} = \frac{1}{2}\left(x_i + \frac{A}{X_i}\right)$$

where A is a positive number,

   x_i is the current approximation of the square root of A,

   x_{i+1} is the next approximation of the square root of A.

Use this formula to find the square root of numbers and stop when:

$$\left| \frac{(x_{i+1})^2 - A}{A} \right| < .001$$

Compare your answers to the results obtained by using the SQRT function.

65. Write programs to find the roots of

$$2X - 1 - 2\sin X = 0$$

using these methods:
(a)   Bisection Method.
(b)   Iteration Method.
(c)   Newton-Raphson Method.

66. (a)   Write a program to solve the following, using Simpson's rule:

$$\int_0^2 \ln\sqrt{1 + x}\ dx$$

(b)   Write a program to solve the following, using the trapezoidal rule:

$$\int_0^{\pi/4} \frac{\sin^a x}{\sqrt{1 + \cos^2 x}}\ dx$$

for $a = 1.0, 1.1, 1.2, ..., 2.0$

ARRAY PROBLEMS

67. Write a program to read in an array of 100 elements. Then count how many groups of three adjacent positive numbers are in the array. Five positive adjacent numbers would mean a count of three.

68. Write a program that reads in a vector of length 30. Each element is to be modified as follows:
    (a) If the value of the element is less than the subscript, square the element.
    (b) If the value of the element is equal to the subscript, reverse the sign of the element.
    (c) If the value of the element is greater than the subscript, subtract one from the element.

69. Write a program to find the determinant of arrays.

70. Write a program that will add arrays of any size. Write a program that will multiply arrays.

INTEREST PROBLEMS

71. Calculate the new balance if $1,000 is deposited at 5% for 10 years with interest compounded quarterly. Next, calculate interest compounded monthly. Finally, calculate interest compounded daily. Compare the results.

72. If an individual wanted to have accumulated $1,000 at the end of 5 years, how much would he have to deposit each year? Assume that the interest rate is 5% compounded yearly and that he makes identical deposits at the first of each year.

73. Manhatten Island was purchased by settlers in 1626 for $24. If the $24 had been deposited in a bank at 6% interest compounded annually, how much would their bank account be worth now?

74. Your bank has a billionaire depositer. Write a program that calculates compound interest (6% compounded monthly) for his account. If he doesn't receive all his interest, he will move his account to another bank and you will lose your job.

75. If a person borrows $500 at 1½% per month, how much has he paid and how much does he still owe after one year if he makes payments of $7.50 per month? How about if he makes payments of $10 per month?

76. Using Problem 75, how many months must the person pay if he pays $10 per month?

BUSINESS PROBLEMS

77. Calculate taxable income by deducting $750 for each dependent and a standard 10% deduction. Read name, social security number, yearly pay, and number of dependents.

78. Write a program to calculate average mileage. Read in starting and stopping speedometer mileage and the number of gallons of gasoline purchased.

79. Since you are poor, you may wish to write a program to analyze your expenses. Write a program to keep track of expenses over three months. Obvious expense categories are food, housing, transportation, entertainment, and educational expenses. Add any other classifications you wish. Then
    (a) Find the total expense for each category for each month.
    (b) Find average expense and the maximum and minimum expense for each category over the three months.

80. Write a check-balancing program for a bank. The master input record consists of:

Customer name	20 characters
Customer account number	5 digits
Present balance	6 digits

Detail transactions consist of:

Customer account number	5 digits
Transaction amount	6 digits

If the transaction is positive, it is a deposit. If the transaction is negative, it is a check. Customers are charged 15¢ for each check they write with a maximum charge of $1. Write a program to balance the accounts, showing all transactions for the bank's customers. If any check would overdraw an account, print a warning message, charge a $3 bad check charge, and don't process the check.

81. Write a program to calculate weekly pay. Read the following data:

Name	20 columns alphabetic
Social security number	9 columns numeric
Number of hours worked	4 column field 99.9
Hourly pay rate	5 column field 99.99
Dependents	2 column field 99

Overtime is paid after 40 hours at 1½ time. Deduct 4% for social security but never deduct more than $10 in one week. Deduct 2% for state tax. Deduct for federal tax according to:

Dependents	Tax Rate
0	16%
1	12%
2	9%
3	6%
4+	5%

Print a report indicating all pertinent information.

82. The READY water company charges these rates:
    .015 per gallon first 100 gallons.
    .011 per gallon after first 100 gallons.
    Write a program to read

Customer name	20 characters
Customer number	4 digits
Last meter reading	4 digits
New meter reading	4 digits

Do calculations necessary to print out:
    Customer name
    Customer number
    Last meter reading
    New meter reading

Amount used
Charges on Rate 1
Charges on Rate 2
Total charges

Stop the program when finding a negative customer number and print totals for:

Total amount used
Total Rate 1
Total Rate 2
Total charges

83. A company bills its customers the last day of each month. If the bill is paid by the 10th of the next month, the customer gets a 1% reduction or $2, whichever is larger. If the bill is paid after the 10th but by the 20th of next month, the customer pays the regular bill. If the bill is paid after the 20th, there is a $1 or 1% service charge, whichever is greater. Write a program to read:

Customer number	5 digits
Date of billing	6 digits month day year
Date of payment	6 digits month day year
Bill amount	XXX.XX
Amount paid	XXX.XX

Calculate the due amount and print any differences between amount paid and amount due.

84. The county property tax office needs assessment totals for the types of land classifications. County tax assessment rates are:

Land Type	Assessment Rate
1	1.01/acre
2	1.21/acre
3	1.49/acre
4	1.87/acre
5	2.31/acre

Each input record contains the following:
Parcel number
Land type
Length in feet
Width in feet

Calculate and print the total assessment for each land parcel (indicate the square feet and acreage). An acre is equal to 43,550 square feet. Next, print summary totals for each land type. Include:
  Land type
  Number of parcels
  Total square feet
  Total acres
  Total assessment
  Percent of all land.

85. The National Losers Society gives out scholarships to campus losers. The minimum requirements are
  (a) C (2.5) grade point average or lower.
  (b) At least a Junior standing (3) or higher.
  (c) Over 30 years old.
  (d) Married—0 unmarried, 1 married.
  Write a program to read the student name (20 columns alphabetic) and the above information, and print all students eligible for awards.

86. A company pays its salesmen 5% commission on total sales less than $1,000 and 6% if total sales are $1,000 or greater. If the salesman has been with the company for over 10 years, he receives an extra 1% commission. Salesmen who have been with the company over 10 years have an even salesman number. Input is a salesman's name, number, and total sales. Calculate the commissions. Print all input and the commissions. Print totals for sales and commissions.

87. A pair of socks cost $1.05 each, or $10.25 a dozen, or $110 a gross. Write a program to calculate the price on sock purchases. For example, 13 socks would cost $11.30 ($10.25 + $1.05). The storekeeper is kind-hearted and wishes to warn his customers whenever they make an unwise purchase. For example, a purchase of 11 pairs of socks costs more than a dozen. Fix the program so it prints a warning message whenever a customer selects an unwise purchase.

88. Write a program to process revolving charge accounts. The data are punched as follows:

Account number	5 digits
Name	20 characters
Street address	20 characters
City-State	20 characters
Zip code	5 digits
Old balance	5 digits
Payments	5 digits
Purchases	5 digits

A service charge of 1½% on any old unpaid balance is charged, with a minimum of 50¢, if there is an unpaid balance. The program should print out new bills to send to the customers.

89. A manufacturer buys a machine with a life of one year to produce consumer goods. Costs are incurred in the production of the goods, and revenue (cash inflow) is generated by the sale of the goods. To calculate the return that the manufacturer earns on his investment, costs are subtracted from revenue to produce a return figure. This return figure is then divided by the initial investment to compute a rate of return.

    Assume that the machine costs $8,000, revenue from sales were $12,000 and the costs incurred, including operating the machine, totalled $10,800. Write a program that calculates return and rate of return, and outputs machine costs, sales, total costs, return, and rate of return. Your output should appear as:

```
Machine
  Cost    Revenue    Costs    Return    Rate
 8000.00  12000.00  10800.00  1200.00   0.15
```

90. Problem 89 must now be expanded to allow the machine (project) to have a life in excess of one year. This modification forces the analyst to deal with uncertainty that results from estimating future magnitudes of sales and costs.

    It is known from analysis of historical data that this machine has a useful life of 10 years; that sales, on the average, grow by 5% a year; and that, on the average, costs increase by 8% per year. Although these percentages are correct in the long run, actions of competitors, economic conditions, and the like tend to make the actual rate of change of costs and sales vary rather drastically from the average rates. The effect of these exogenous forces can be simulated by using a random number generator to modify the average annual changes in cost and sales. Although rather marked variations will occur, the net effect of inclusion of the random variation will be zero.

Since it is reasonable to assume that the changes in sales and costs are related, only one random number should be generated for each year. This number would be multiplied by the average change in sales and costs to produce the simulated change in the variables for a given year. The random numbers should have values between 0.5 and 1.5.

Add to the output of Problem 89 the year numbers down the left-hand column of the page. Note that the output for year one is the same as the output of Problem 89.

91. The simple rate of return approach used in Problem 90 is not satisfactory to some managers. An approach which has gained institutional although not academic acceptance is payback period analysis. This technique computes the time necessary to recoup an initial investment.

The payback computation must take a cumulative form. That is, each year's return (cash inflows) is accumulated until the initial investment has been fully covered. For example, assume an initial investment of $31,000 and net cash inflows in the succeeding years of $10,000, $20,000, $10,000, and $10,000, respectively.

Year	Cash Outlay	Net Cash Flows Each Year	Accumulated
0	31,000	- -	- -
1	- -	10,000	10,000
2	- -	20,000	30,000
3	- -	10,000	31,000
4	- -	10,000	- -

In this instance, assuming payments occur uniformly over each year, analysis of the third year reveals that the final $1,000 needed to recoup the investment would occur after one-tenth of the year. Consequently, the payback period for this investment is 2.1 years.

Compute the payback period for the machine purchase analyzed in Problem 90. Your output should include the complete results of Problem 90 plus an additional line as output of the payback period.

92. Expand Problem 91 to include many investments. The basic data for each of the investments has been keypunched on data cards in the following layout:

Card Columns	Content
1-2	Machine number
3-4	Number of periods
5-14	Initial outlay = Machine cost
15-24	Sales
25-34	Costs
35-44	Change in sales
45-54	Change in cost

It is possible that erroneously punched cards were not all removed from the data deck; hence, your program must check for the validity of the data. Invalid data are defined as follows:

(a) A machine number less than or equal to zero, or greater than 10.

(b) A number of periods for the investment less than or equal to zero, or greater than 15.

(c) An initial outlay smaller than $1,000.

(d) An initial sales estimate which is less than an initial cost estimate.

If any of these invalid conditions exist, the whole data card should be ignored and your program should read another data card. The end of the data deck is signalled by an end-of-data card with an investment number of 99 and a number of periods of 99. Your output should appear as follows:

Investment number	2
Number of periods	10
Initial outlay	8000.00
Initial sales	12000.00
Initial cost	10800.00
Rate of change for sales	0.050
Rate of change for costs	0.080

PERIOD	SALES	Cost	RETURN	RATE
1	12000.00	10800.00	1200.00	0.15
2	12127.42	10983.49	1143.93	0.14
3	11995.32	10792.05	1203.26	0.15
4	11538.07	10133.84	1404.22	0.18
5	12457.86	11426.41	1031.45	0.13
6	12536.89	11542.39	994.50	0.12
7	12600.14	11635.56	964.57	0.12
8	13096.13	12368.40	727.73	0.09
9	13919.05	13611.91	307.14	0.04
10	13540.53	13019.64	520.88	0.07

Payback period   7.08

93. Refer to Problem 92. Instead of computing values for the return in a given year from sales and cost estimates, assume that future returns themselves have been estimated and keypunched. A data deck has been prepared that includes project data and the associated future returns.

   The first type (of which there is only one) contains the project data in the following layout. Validity checking is not necessary.

Card Column	Content
1-2	Project number
3-4	Life of project
5-14	Initial outlay with the decimal point punched

The second type (of which there are an unknown number) contains the estimated returns:

Card Column	Content
1-2	Year number
3-12	Return with the decimal point punched

These cards (type two) have to be checked for validity. Invalid conditions are defined as follows:
(a) A year number less than or equal to zero.
(b) A year number greater than the life of the project.
(c) A return value less than zero.

The end of the data deck is indicated by an end-of-data-card with a year number of 99.

Note that since the year number is punched on the data card, there is no need to have cards in order. Your program should read a type-two data card, test it for validity and assign the return value to a one-dimensional array so that the position of the value in the array corresponds to the year in which that return will be earned. Although it is unlikely that any project will have a life of 99 years, it is suggested that the array for storing returns be dimensioned 99 so as to allow for all possibilities. If a data card does not exist for a given year, the return for that year should be assigned a value of zero.

After all the values have been assigned, print out only that part of the array that pertains to the life of the project and payback period for the project. The output should appear as follows:

```
 1          8      16000.00
 4                  3600.00
 3                  1900.00
12                  8000.00
 1                  1000.00
 7                  6300.00
 6                  6700.00
 8                  5200.00
 5                 -1400.00
 5                  5400.00
99                     0.00
```

PERIOD	RETURN	RATE
1	1000.00	0.06
2	0.00	0.00
3	1900.00	0.12
4	3600.00	0.22
5	5400.00	0.34
6	6700.00	0.42
7	6300.00	0.39
8	5200.00	0.32
Payback period	5.61	

94. The Local Gas Company bills its customers according to these rates:

First	500 cubic feet	$1.10
Next	3,000 cubic feet	0.130 per hundred
Next	32,000 cubic feet	0.125 per hundred
Next	100,000 cubic feet	0.120 per hundred
Next	150,000 cubic feet	0.100 per hundred
Next	400,000 cubic feet	0.095 per hundred
Next	685,500 cubic feet	0.087 per hundred

The input record has these fields:

Name	16 characters
Street address	16 characters
City-State	16 characters
Meter begin	7 digits
Meter end	7 digits
Date from	6 digits
Date to	6 digits
Meter number	6 digits

Write a program to prepare bills for the gas company.

CHANGE PROBLEMS

95. Write a program that makes change with the rule that one is always given the fewest number of coins. For example, if you give the grocer $1.00 for a 21¢ item he will give you back a fifty-cent piece, a quarter, and four pennies.

96. Write a program to print the number of different ways a dollar bill can be broken into change. Assume there are pennies, nickels, dimes, quarters, and half-dollars.

97. The old English currency system used pounds, shillings (12 shillings = pound), and pence (20 pence = shilling). Write a program for a cash register that accepts a payment amount and purchase price, and then calculates correct change.

CALENDAR PROBLEMS

A year is a leap year (that is, February has 29 days instead of 28 days) if it is a multiple of 4, except that a multiple of 100 is a leap year only if it is also a multiple of 400. January 1, 1800, was a Wednesday.

98. Write a program that reads any date (month, day, year) and prints the day of the week.

99. Write a program to find the next three-day weekend caused by the 4th of July.

100. (a) Write a program to generate a calendar for the present year.
   (b) Write a program to read two dates and calculate how many days have passed.

101. Friday the 13th.
   (a) What is the probability of the 13th of the month being a Friday?
   (b) Write a program to count how many Friday the 13th's occur in this century.
   (c) Why is the 13th of the month more likely to be a Friday than any one of the other days of the week?

Appendix I

Program Rewriting

It is almost a truism that every program can be shortened. The following examples demonstrate a particular case, but the techniques are applicable to many programs. The discussion is based on Simpson's rule for numerical integration. This very simple problem was chosen to illustrate the point of shortening source programs. It is unlikely that such a trivial case would exist in actuality.

$$\int_{x_0}^{x_n} x \, dx = \frac{h}{3} (x_0 + 4x_1 + 2x_2 + 4x_3 + 2x_4 + \ldots + 2x_{n-2}$$

$$+ 4x_{n-1} + x_n)$$

where $x_{i+1} = x_i + h$.

Example: $\int_1^5 x \, dx$

Choosing $h = .5$

$$\int_1^5 x \, dx = \frac{.5}{3} (1 + 4(1.5) + 2(2) + 4(2.5) + 2(3) + 4(3.5) + 2(4)$$

$$+ 4(4.5) + 5) = 12$$

The following seven examples progressively shorten the program. Upon investigation, program 5 is larger, from the standpoint of core

224

requirements, than several of the less elegant cases even though it does not seem to be so. Program 6 is a different approach entirely and is the shortest and best of all those presented. Program 7 is an example of going too far with this technique. Though the source program is the shortest (in number of statements), the number of object instructions executed is very high for large $(x_n - x_0)$ and/or small h.

PROGRAM 1

```
      SUBROUTINE INTGR(XZERO,XSUBN, H, SUM)
      A=XZERO
      B=XSUBN
      HOVR3=H/3.
      I=1
      SUM=A+B
1     A=A+H
      GO TO (2,4),I
2     SUM=SUM+4.*A
      IF(A-(B-H))3,6,6
3     I=2
      GO TO 1
4     SUM=SUM+2.*A
      IF(A-(B-H))5,6,6
5     I=1
      GO TO 1
6     SUM=SUM*HOVR3
      RETURN
      END
```

Note: There is no requirement to introduce the variables A, B, and HOVR3. They serve only to lengthen the program. The testing (IF(A-(B-H))) is clumsy and badly placed in the text.

PROGRAM 2

```
       SUBROUTINE INTGR(XZERO, XSUBN, H, SUM)
       I=1
       SUM=XZERO+XSUBN
       XZERO=XZERO+H
  1    GO TO (2,4), I
  2    SUM=SUM+4.*XZERO
       I=2
  3    XZERO=XZERO+H
       IF(XZERO-XSUBN)1,5,5
  4    SUM=SUM+2.*XZERO
       I=1
       GO TO 3
  5    SUM=SUM*H/3.
       RETURN
       END
```

Note: The extraneous variables have been removed and the test for completion is less clumsy, but the presence of a pair of two identical statements (XZERO = XZERO + H, I = 1) implies that a further rearrangement is possible. One should always be wary of a program that repeats identical statements.

PROGRAM 3

```
       SUBROUTINE INTGR(XZERO, XSUBN, H, SUM)
       SUM=XZERO+XSUBN
  1    I=1
  2    XZERO=XZERO+H
       IF(XZERO-XSUBN)3,6,6
  3    GO TO (4,5), I
  4    SUM=SUM+4.*XZERO
       I=2
       GO TO 2
  5    SUM=SUM+2.*XZERO
       GO TO 1
  6    SUM=SUM*H/3.
       RETURN
       END
```

Note: By rearrangement of statements, we have eliminated one appearance of XZERO = XZERO + H , and I = 1, However, the similarity between SUM = SUM + 4. *XZERO and SUM = SUM + 2. *XZERO is now suspect.

PROGRAM 4

```
    SUBROUTINE INTGR(XZERO, XSUBN, H, SUM)
    SUM=XZERO+XSUBN
1   A=4
    I=1
2   XZERO=XZERO+H
    IF(XZERO-XSUBN)3,5,5
3   SUM=SUM+A*XZERO
    GO TO (4,1),I
4   I=2
    A=2.
    GO TO 2
5   SUM=SUM*H/3.
    RETURN
    END
```

Note: The two similar (but not identical) statements of program 3 have been modified so that now a single statement SUM = SUM + A *XZERO appears with A alternately 2 and 4. Now, however, note the similarity between SUM = SUM + A *XZERO and SUM = XZERO + XSUBN in that a special case is required for the first and last points of the series.

PROGRAM 5

```
    SUBROUTINE INTGR(XZERO, XSUBN, H, SUM)
    SUM=0.
1   A=1.
2   I=1
3   SUM=SUM+A*XZERO
    XZERO=XZERO+H
    IF(XZERO-XSUBN)4,1,7
4   GO TO (5,6), I
5   I=2
    A=4.
    GO TO 3
```

```
6   A=2.
    GO TO 2
7   SUM=SUM*H/3.
    RETURN
    END
```

Note: Although we have succeeded in reducing the principal arithmetic to one statement (SUM = SUM + A *XZERO), the extraneous control arithmetic necessary for proper functioning makes this case less desirable than program 4.

PROGRAM 6

```
    SUBROUTINE INTGR(XZERO, XSUBN, H, SUM)
    A=1.
    SUM=XZERO+XSUBN
1   XZERO=XZERO+H
    IF(XZERO-XSUBN) 2,3,3
2   SUM=SUM+(3.+A)*XZERO
    A=-A
    GO TO 1
3   SUM=SUM*H/3.
    RETURN
    END
```

Note: A total change of direction here has produced the best program so far.

PROGRAM 7

```
    SUBROUTINE INTGR (XZERO, XSUBN, H, SUM)
    A = 1.
    SUM = H/3. * (XZERO + XSUBN)
1   XZERO = XZERO + H
    SUM = SUM + (H/3.) * (3. + A) * XZERO
    A = -A
    IF(XZERO + H -XSUBN) 1, 2, 2
2   RETURN
    END
```

Note: From the standpoint of length, this program is less satisfactory than number 6.   From the standpoint of the number of object in-instructions executed, it is extremely poor. Note that $(H/3)$ is a multiplicative constant for *every* execution of the statement SUM = SUM + (H/3) * (3 + A) * XZERO

Comparative Analysis of Programs 1 – 7

	1	2	3	4	5	6	7
Real variables	7	4	4	5	5	5	5
Real constants	3	3	3	3	5	2	2
Integer variables	1	1	1	1	1	0	0
Integer constants	2	2	2	2	2	0	0
Statement numbers	6	5	6	5	7	3	2
Number of floating-point operations	19	16	14	13	13	15	17
Number of fixed-point operations	3	3	2	2	2	0	0
IFs	2	1	1	1	1	1	1
GO TOs	2	1	2	1	2	1	0
Computed GO TOs	1	1	1	1	1	0	0

Reprinted from *1130 FORTRAN Programming Techniques.*   C20-1642. IBM Corp.

Appendix II

FETE

A FORTRAN EXECUTION TIME ESTIMATOR

by
Daniel H. H. Ingalls

INTRODUCTION

If you want to live cheaply, you must make a list of how much money is spent on each thing every day. This enumeration will quickly reveal the principal areas of waste. The same method works for saving computer time. Originally, one had to put his own timers and counters into a program to determine the distribution of time spent in each part. Recently several automated systems have appeared which either insert counters automatically or interrupt the program during its execution to produce the tallies. FETE is a system of the former type which has two outstanding characteristics: it is very easy to implement and it is very easy to use. By demonstrating such convenience, it should establish execution timing as a standard tool in program development.

FETE is a three-step process. The first step accepts any FORTRAN (IV) program such as the example in Fig. A2.1 and produces an edited file with counters. The second step executes the modified program, but retains the source file. After execution, the third step re-reads the modified source and correlates it with the final counter values to provide the listing shown in Fig. A2.2. Here the executable statements have been collected and appear beside the exact number of executions and approximate computation time. The number of TRUE branches of logical IFs is tallied on the right, and subtotals appear at the end of each routine timed.

*Stanford University. STAN-CS-71-204.

```
C       PRINT OUT FIRST 100 PRIMES
        INTEGER PRIMES(100)
        PRIMES(1) = 2
        PRIMES(2) = 3
        N = 3
        DO 30 INDEX=3,100
C       GET NEXT (ODD) CANDIDATE
10      N = N + 2
C       RUN THROUGH POSSIBLE (PRIME) DIVISORS
        K = 2
20      IQUOTN = N/PRIMES(K)
        IF(PRIMES(K)*IQUOTN.EQ.N) GO TO 10
        IF(IQUOTN.LE.PRIMES(K)) GO TO 30
        K = K + 1
        GO TO 20
30      PRIMES(INDEX) = N
        WRITE(6,40) PRIMES
40      FORMAT('1 THE FIRST 100 PRIMES ARE:',I3(/8I10))
        STOP
        END
```

Figure A2.1. Listing of sample program to be timed.

EXECUTABLE STATEMENTS	EXECUTIONS	COST	TRUE
PRIMES(1) = 2	1	2	
PRIMES(2) = 3	1	2	
N = 3	1	1	
DO 30 INDEX=3,100	1	2	
10 N = N + 2	269	538	
K = 2	269	269	
20 IQUOTN = N/PRIMES(K)	911	8199	
IF(PRIMES(K)*IQUOTN.EQ.N) GO TO 10	911	7459	171
IF(IQUOTN.LE.PRIMES(K)) GO TO 30	740	2318	98
K = K + 1	642	1284	
GO TO 20	642	642	
30 PRIMES(INDEX) = N	98	294	
WRITE(6,40) PRIMES	1	506	
STOP	1	0	
END			
SUBTOTALS FOR THIS ROUTINE - - -	4757	21516	
***** 16 EXECUTABLE, 2 NON-EX, 3 COMMENTS; TOTALS:	4757	21516	

Figure A2.2. Sample program timed. Only executable statements are displayed.

THE VALUE OF EXECUTION TIME PROFILES

The second section of this paper will show how such a format for execution time feedback may be easily achieved. This first section jumps ahead to treat the implications of this tool for computer programming in general. The style may follow that of a patent medicine dealer describing his special brand of panacea, but the enthusiasm comes mainly from watching sceptical programmers using FETE for the first time.

Execution-time profiles are of value in three main areas of programming: improving old programs, writing new programs, and educating programmers. In improvement of old programs it most often happens that the programmer initially does not know what the program does. Even when improving one's own program, much of the original scheme has probably faded from memory (and we all know how much the comments will help). The results of the appendix show that from a typical program, approximately 3% of the code constitutes 50% of the execution time. In some sense, then, we may conclude that if a naive programmer sets out to improve a program, he will work 30 times more effectively if he has a FETE (or similar) listing in front of him. Two words describe the programmers I have watched looking at their FETE runs: focused attention. The human mind's most powerful tool is selective attention, but the selection requires an awareness about the environment which in this situation is furnished by a source-level presentation of execution time distribution.

Since FETE became operational, I have changed my own approach to programming. My three steps to creating a program used to be:

1 Think how I want to do it.
2 Write it up in the best way.
3 Debug it.

The numbers at the left are not to indicate order but are an estimate of how long the steps take. My new recipe is more like the following:

1 Think how I want to do it.
1 Write it up in the quickest way.

1   Debug it.
0   Get a FETE listing.
1   Rewrite and debug the important parts.

The writing time is less because you assume that none of the program needs to be efficient (remember that only 3% does). The debugging time is less because the code you have to debug is really simple. The time to rewrite the important sections is low because although you try to write very efficient code, there is very little which needs this attention. The result is a program written in two-thirds the time, and which is much easier to understand because it is simply written. On top of that, it probably runs faster, because the inner loops have been specially written. The first run of FETE upon itself led to a twofold increase in speed!

The instructional value of execution-time awareness must be great. For one thing, the programmer will learn to recognize inefficient algorithms. Moreover, the reinforcement from FETE enhances the aesthetic enjoyment of writing a good program. The nicest reward which came from finishing FETE was being able to run it on itself, in part because it was fun to improve, and part because it was clear when the job was finished. Many people point out that good programs come from good algorithms, yet the implication is often that only programmers such as the critic are capable of choosing good algorithms. My feeling is that much mediocre programming comes about only because the programmer is lost in his program and can't see what is important. He would choose better methods if he had better perspective, and that is exactly what FETE and similar systems can provide.

The current approach to higher level languages aims at liberating the programmer from petty (hardware and archaic software) considerations. This is a laudable goal, but one must not include computation as a petty consideration. APL is a good example of a liberating language, but it also masks the huge amount of processing behind much of its vocabulary. The risk of conciseness is that a bad algorithm may fit on one line, and never be noticed. Incorporation of execution-time tallies into the new languages offers a solution to this problem, by maintaining the awareness of the programmer at the same level as the power of the language. Those contemplating new compilers would do well to include execution time profiles as an option for users.

IMPLEMENTING SOURCE-LEVEL EXECUTION PROFILES

As summarized in the introduction, FETE is a three-step procedure. Since the second step runs as a normal FORTRAN job it entails no effort other than job-control organization. The bulk of this section is devoted to describing the details of the first and third phases of FETE.

Figure A2.3 shows the modified source produced from the program of Fig. A2.1 during FETE's first step. The annotations (a) through (l) refer to Fig. A2.3. The first insertion (a) is a labelled common declaration for the counter array. The dimension 2000 is adequate for most programs up to 6000 statements in length. The common declaration is inserted in all subprograms immediately following any SUBROUTINE, FUNCTION, or IMPLICIT statements. The names KOUNT1, KOUNT3, etc., are unlikely to conflict with users' names as they are spelled with a zero, not an O. Initialization of the counters (b) occurs immediately before the first "noticeably" executable statement (a nonarithmetic executable statement). FETE makes no attempt to recognize statement functions because of the difficulty of inserting counters for them, and hence must assume that the first arithmetic statements might have been function definitions. The first counter must then be inserted (c) to tally the executions of any preceding arithmetic statements. From here on, counters need be inserted only where control branches and where logical IFs occur. For instance, we need counters immediately after a DO statement (d) because there is an implied loop entry at that point. Now note what became of statement 10. FETE removes each statement label (except those which terminate DO-loops), and attaches it to an inserted counter (e). In this way, each time control branches into the main line of code, the extra executions will be recorded. If a CONTINUE statement is stripped of its label in this way, it will be deleted from the source, and a flag set in the counter so that it may be recreated for the final listing.

When FETE encounters a logical IF, it first strips off the target statement and replaces it by a counter. The resulting IF statement is then inserted (f) above the original. Thus, even if the original IF would cause a branch out of line, the fact that the branch was taken will be recorded by the counter. Usually the editing of IFs can be done on one line, as is the case in our example; however, when the IF

i	j	k	l
0		1	0
027	1	1	2
1	1	1	2
1	1	1	1
0			
0			
5			
1	2	2	2
5			
6	1	2	2
1	1	2	2
1	1	2	1
6	1	2	9
1	1	2	9
3	4	2	8
3	4	2	3
1	1	2	2
1	4	2	1
2	1	2	3
5			
118			1506
033			1506
0			
1	7	1	0
721	0		3

```fortran
a)      COMMON /KOUNT2/ KOUNT5(2000),KOUNT3
        INTEGER PRIMES(100)
        PRIMES(1) = 2
        PRIMES(2) = 3
        N = 3
b)      DO 83294 KOUNT3=1,2000
83294   KOUNT5(KOUNT3)=0
c)      KOUNT5(   1)=KOUNT5(   1)+1
        DO 30 INDEX=3,100
d)      KOUNT5(   2)=KOUNT5(   2)+1
e)      KOUNT5(   3)=KOUNT5(   3)+1
        N = N + 2
10      K = 2
20      KOUNT5(   4)=KOUNT5(   4)+1
        IQUOTN = N/PRIMES(K)
f)      IF(PRIMES(K)*IQUOTN.EQ.N)         KOUNT5(   5)=KOUNT5(   5)+15
        IF(PRIMES(K)*IQUOTN.EQ.N) GO TO 10
        IF(IQUOTN.LE.PRIMES(K))           KOUNT5(   6)=KOUNT5(   6)+15
        IF(IQUOTN.LE.PRIMES(K)) GO TO 30
        K = K + 1
        GO TO 20
30      PRIMES(INDEX) = N
g)      KOUNT5(   7)=KOUNT5(   7)+1
        WRITE(6,40) PRIMES
40      FORMAT('1 THE FIRST 100 PRIMES ARE:',13(/8I10))
h)      CALL KOUNT1
        STOP
        END
```

Figure A2.3. Sample program edited by FETE. Lower case letters refer to text.

clause is too long (typically less than 5% of the time), appropriate continuation cards are generated from the IF-counter. Most of the time, FETE does not insert counters after IF statements. Almost all target statements of IFs are either arithmetic or GO TOs. In the former case, the main-line execution count will be unchanged; in the latter, it must be decreased by the value of the IF counter (i.e., the number of branches out of line. The analysis routine which reads the counters can determine which was the case by examining the sequence-column flags (q.v.). In indeterminate cases, such as a CALL with multiple returns, or a READ with ERR return, FETE inserts a counter after the IF to be safe.

Note (g) of Fig. A2.2 indicates a labelled statement which has not been modified in the manner of the other labelled statements. The terminal statement of a DO-loop presents a special problem to execution tallying. On the one hand we need a labelled counter before the statement in question for the tallies and so that transfers to the label will work properly; yet that would end the DO-loop above the statement originally labelled, and exclude it from the loop. Fortunately, though, we have enough extra information to solve the dilemma. The following simplified code segment illustrates the situation:

```
        . . .
        K(n)   = K(n)+1
        DO 10 I = I1,I2
        K(n+1) = K(n+1)+1
        . . .
   10   P(I) = F
        K(n+2) = K(n+2)+1
        . . .
```

One thing we know for sure: K(n+1) would have the correct tally for statement 10 if there were no branches out of the DO-loop. In fact if we could subtract from K(n+1) the number of branches out of the DO-loop, then we would have the answer. Now we note that the only way for K(n) to be stepped without K(n+2) increasing also is if there is a branch out of the loop. Thus we obtain our result that P(I) = F must have been executed $K(n+1) - K(n) + K(n+2)$ times. The interested reader may deduce the result for a statement which terminates two nested DO-loops with the same end-label.

When FETE encounters a STOP (or CALL EXIT or RETURN in the main program) it inserts a call (h) to the analysis routine (KOUNT1) which goes back to correlate the modified source with the counter contents. Provision is also made for termination in an IF statement such as

IF (NCARD.EQ.LAST) STOP

Here the IF clause will be repeated three times; once with a counter, once with a CALL, and a last time with the STOP.

FETE handles SUBROUTINES and FUNCTIONS in the same manner as the MAIN, except that no counter initialization is inserted and a RETURN is not treated as a STOP. We move on now to deal with the sequence-column flags before summarizing the task of the analysis routine.

The sequence column fields of Fig. A2.3 are denoted i, j, k, l. Field j is a two-digit code for the statement type (1 = arithmetic, 2 = DO, 3 = IF, 4 = GO TO, etc.). Since logical IFs are flagged in the i-field, their j-field is used to give the classification of the target statement. The k-field is a two-digit index of the depth of DO-nesting. Actually, this value does not increase with every DO encountered, but only when the DO refers to an end-label not yet used in previous DOs. The convention economizes on stack space, and yet gives enough information to the analysis routine. The l-field gives the "cost" of each statement, and is responsible for the 'dirty' in FETE's designation as a quick-and-dirty system. FETE determines cost by a linear scan of each executable statement which looks for operators, parentheses, etc., charging a reasonable fee for each. Another base cost is derived from the statement type, and the operator cost is then added on. In statements such as WRITE or FUNCTION, a further charge is levied for each comma encountered to reflect the extra argument overhead. At each left-parenthesis a check is made to see if the preceding identifier was a FORTRAN internal function name, and if so the appropriate cost is added on from a table.

Most of the cost of a CALL is put into the corresponding SUBROUTINE statement. The justification is a human engineering consideration, to suggest to a programmer the possibility of writing his subroutine in line to save time. To evaluate that suggestion, the programmer really wants to see the total cost of the subroutine linkage in one number, rather than in five calls scattered throughout his program. The same convention is especially appropriate for FUNCTION statements, because FETE's lack of a symbol table precludes detection of the implied calls, yet the tallies in the function code will be correct.

Future versions of FETE will use a more elegant cost assessment, but this crude scheme has been remarkably successful. The source editing is performed in one pass without scratch files, and takes roughly one-fifth as long as the FORTRAN compilation.

The analysis routine, which comprises FETE's third phase, is linked in during the FORTRAN step, so that it may be called just before the program would have come to a STOP. This phase rereads the modified source and correlates the executable statements with the counter values and prints the FETE listing in one last pass.

The *i*-field of the sequence-column flags was originally intended as a coded column of useful facts for the analysis routine. However, as that routine took shape, it became clear that these numbers worked as op-codes for an analysis-machine. This is one of several instances where I have found new insight into a problem by considering its data-to-program relationship to be a form of program-to-machine relationship. I have chosen to lay this on the reader by roughly outlining the order code of the analysis machine in Table A2.1 and inviting him to simulate the analysis of this sample program.

As the analysis routine proceeds through the file, it maintains subtotals and totals of executions and cost and prints these for the programmer to use for judging relative importance of different parts of the listing. Percentage cost is not given for two reasons. First is the necessity for an extra pass through the source file (or a smaller file with static costs only). Second is the observation that people using FETE simply scan the cost column visually for the number of digits, a process for which FETE's large integers are ideally suited. A simple statistic which I included out of curiosity is the running total of the executions and costs squared. From these and the normal totals, the r.m.s. values may be compared with the mean values to give an idea of how "peaky" the execution and cost are. All of these statistics are currently printed out in a table for instrumentation curiosity, and some results gathered from 17 sample programs appear in the appendix.

The FETE approach to determining actual timing is a very coarse one, but has proved to be 90% effective in giving programmers what

Table A2.1. Order Code of the Analysis Machine. Initial conditions are ISFRST = YES and IK = 1. Tallying is described in text.

i-field	Operation	Comment
0	If *j* not blank, then tally static. Set ISEXEC = NO.	Not executable or not from original source.
1	Dynamic count is KOUNT5(IK); Tally static, dynamic, and by cost; Set ISEXEC = YES; Print with counts; If *k* = 2, push 0 onto D0-stack if new D0-label, then add KOUNT5(IK+1)−KOUNT5(IK) to top of D0-stack; if *k* = 21 (END), then print subtotals and set ISFRST= YES.	Executable statement.
2.	Dynamic count is KOUNT5(IK+1) + top of D0-stack; pop D0-stack; proceed otherwise as when *i* = 1.	End of a D0-loop.
3	IF count is KOUNT5(IK−1); TRUE count is KOUNT5(IK); if *j* = 1, then move KOUNT5(IK−1) into KOUNT5(IK); if *j* = 4, then move KOUNT5(IK−1)−KOUNT5(IK) into KOUNT5(IK); Proceed otherwise as when *i* = 1.	Logical IF.
4	If ISEXEC print with counts.	Continuation card.
5	If not ISFRST, IK = IK+1; set ISFRST = NO.	Inserted counter.
6	Save label and append to next line with *i* ¬ = 4; If *j* = 12, create CONTINUE statement as next line; proceed as when *i* = 5.	Labelled counter.
7	Print END followed by subtotals and totals; Number source comments is 1000 * *k* +1; Print table of statistics; RETURN.	Last statement of program.

they want.   Other workers have developed compilers incorporating
the whole execution-timing process, and that is obviously the proper
approach.   With the symbol table available, the timing of Input/
Output statements can be assessed, the code-generator can give exact
timings for the other statements, and the insertion of counters is
efficient, both in placement and in code generated.   Furthermore,
the compiler's run-time routines can usually pick up the pieces after
a program dies or runs out of time, and the FETE enumeration of
executions would be informative in such cases.

FETE has proved to be very useful at Stanford.   A version to
work with WATFIV allows inexpensive timing for use on the level of
student programming assignments.   The morality of enhancing FOR-
TRAN may be suspect, but hopefully the optimistic results described
here will inspire availability of execution time profiles in all languages before any damage is done.

APPENDIX—PROGRAM LOCALIZATION

A phenomenon of considerable interest is the manner in which
programs tend to spend all their time in a very small portion of their
total code.   The first version of FETE included instrumentation for
investigating the effect, and this appendix describes the results.

Let us suppose that we have an N-statement program of which only
k statements are significant, and these are equal in cost.   The fraction
of statements required to make up 50% of the execution time of this
program would be $k/2N$.   Letting $c(j)$ be the cost of the jth statement, we can define a mean cost M and a root-mean-square cost, as

$$M = \frac{1}{N} \sum_{j=1}^{N} c(j) \qquad R = \sqrt{\frac{1}{N} \sum_{j=1}^{N} c^2(j)}$$

where the summations are overall statements of the program.   For our
hypothetical program, we may let $c = T/k$ for k of the statements and
$c = 0$ for the other $N-k$ statements, so that $M = T/N$ and $R = T\sqrt{kN}$.
I now tentatively define the Ingalls factor $I = M^2/2R^2$, which should
give the number of statements making up 50% of execution time.
Such a definition for I is motivated by the observation that r.m.s./
mean measures how 'peaky' a function is over the interval considered.

Figure A2.A1 shows a plot of the tentative *I*-factor against the actual 50% factor for 17 randomly selected programs. These varied in size from 100 to 3,500 cards and in content from numerical integration to a meta-compiler. Both the linearity and the uniformity of the points over the sample programs are striking. Departure of the slope from unity is due to the invalid assumption that all significant statements have equal weight. Redefining the *I*-factor as $I = 0.4 \; M^2/R^2$, we have an empirically good measure of program localization. Moreover, the plot shows a value of 3% to be typical. Without a more detailed study of program graphs, this statistic does not imply much about how programs should be partitioned. However, the 3% figure does demonstrate the enormous potential of source-level timings for focusing attention on inner loops.

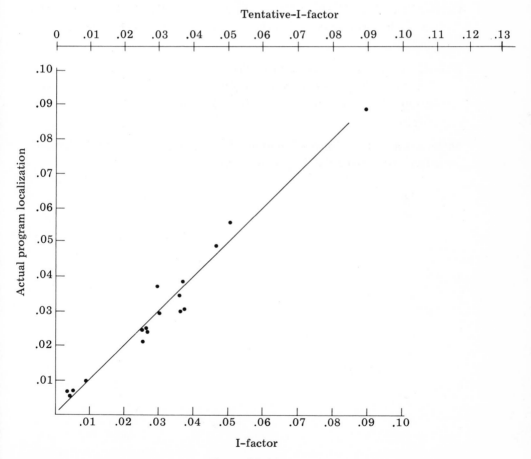

Figure A2.A1

FETE grew out of a research project in programming languages led by Donald Knuth and supported by IBM Corporation, Xerox Corporation and ARPA. I am also indebted to Dick Sweet at Stanford for the FORTRAN statement classifier used in FETE.

Bibliography

Cerf, V. G. "Measurement of Recursive Programs." Ph.D. Thesis, School of Engineering and Applied Science, University of California, Los Angeles, California, Report 70-43, May 1970, 106 pp.

Conrow, K., and Smith, R. "NEATER2: A PL/I Source Statement Reformatter," *CACM*, Vol. 13 No. 11 (1970), pp. 669-675.

Darden, Stephen C., and Heller, Steven B. "Streamline your software development," *Computer Decisions 2* (October 1970), 29-33.

Russell, E. C., Jr. "Automatic Program Analysis." Ph.D. Thesis, School of Engineering and Applied Science, University of California, Los Angeles, California, Report 69-12, March 1969, 168 pp.

Satterthwaite, E. "Source Language Debugging Tools." Ph.D. Thesis, Stanford University, in preparation.

Appendix III

Optimization of Tape Operations*

By Selection of Mathematically
Correct Blocking Factors

by
Ewing S. Walker

Recent technical articles on computer operating efficiency concern themselves primarily with languages, operating system configuration, disk accessing methods and memory size. Tape methodology is largely undiscussed, although the largest amount of data is still retained and processed with tape systems. The fact that a $30 reel of tape can retain as much data as five $300 disk packs clearly establishes the use of tape storage for data that is accessed only on a monthly or weekly cycle.

Optimization of tape I/O time can be achieved via selection of blocking factors using the calculus of variations. This method involves the minimization of the number of interblock gaps on the input and output tapes of the program being optimized. This minimization of interblock gaps will reduce the time wasted to pass the read/write head across the interblock gap. This is lost time to the channel and the tape drive.

As the following formula for I.B.M. 2401-V tape drives indicates, 7.38 milliseconds are required for the read/write head to cross this interblock gap, while .0083 millisecond is required to read a character of data.

Time per block = $7.38 + .0083N$ milliseconds where N = characters/block

Time per file = (Number of blocks) $((7.38) + .0083N)$

Software Age. August/September, 1970.

To illustrate the importance of blocking factors, a file of 300,000 card images on tape can be read in 420 seconds if blocked 10, while if blocked 30 it can be read in 273 seconds.

Blocked 30

$$\text{Time in ms} = 10,000 \ (7.38 + .0083 \ (2400))$$
$$= 273 \text{ seconds}$$

Blocked 10

$$\text{Time in ms} = 30,000 \ (7.38 + .0083 \ (800))$$
$$= 420 \text{ seconds}$$

To fully optimize I/O time, this tape file should contain one block, theoretically. That is, the entire file should be one record. (Error recovery considerations would make this blocking factor unrealistic.) This would require a 24 million byte memory buffer. Therefore the methodology is to minimize the number of interblock gaps, constrained only by the memory available which can easily be determined after program compilation. Therefore mathematically:

$$(\text{Number of blocks}) = \frac{\text{Records/File}}{\text{Records/Block}} = \text{Minimum}$$

where Records/file is known and Records/Block is unknown and to be determined mathematically.

Memory Equation Constraint

$$(\text{Bytes Available}) = \left(\frac{\text{Bytes}}{\text{Record}} \times \frac{\text{Records}}{\text{Block}} \right) + \\ \text{File 1}$$

$$\cdots + \left(\frac{\text{Bytes}}{\text{Record}} \times \frac{\text{Records}}{\text{Block}} \right) \\ \text{File } N$$

For a relatively standard history update program consisting of history input, transaction input, updated history output, and a report file, the method of optimization is illustrated in Fig. A3.1.

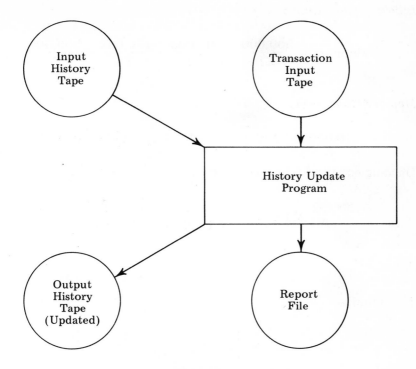

Figure A3.1

Assume for the sake of the example that the history input and output both contain approximately 500,000 150-byte records, the transaction input contains 100,000 80-byte records, output report tape 200,000 70-byte records.

For memory allocation, assume that 10,000 bytes are available for buffer areas with alternate areas reserved.

Then, the memory equation:

Memory

$$10,000 = 2\,(150\,\underset{\text{Record}}{\underline{\text{Bytes}\;(X1)}} + 150\,(X2)\;+$$

(over the terms above: *History-In*   *History-Out*)

$$80\,(X3) + 70\,(X4))$$

(over the terms above: *TRANS-IN*   *Report-Out*)

Where $X1$, $X2$, $X3$, $X4$ are Records/Block for files 1, 2, 3, 4.

Blocking Gap Minimum

$$\text{Minimum} = \frac{500,000}{X1} + \frac{500,000}{X2} + \frac{100,000}{X3} + \frac{200,000}{X4} \qquad \text{(I)}$$

Memory Constraint

$$10,000 = 300\ X1 + 300\ X2 + 160\ X3 + 140\ X4 \qquad \text{(II)}$$

Dividing equation (I) by 100,000 leaves

$$\text{Minimum} = \frac{5}{X1} + \frac{5}{X2} + \frac{1}{X3} + \frac{2}{X4}$$

Solution

To minimize

$$F(Xi) = \frac{5}{X1} + \frac{5}{X2} + \frac{1}{X3} + \frac{2}{X4}$$

Under equality constraint

$$\Phi = 300X1 + 300X2 + 160X3 + 140X4 - 10,000$$

Using LaGrange multiplier technique

$$\frac{\partial F(Xi)}{\partial Xi} + \frac{\lambda \partial \Phi}{\partial Xi} = 0$$

The partial differentiation will result in the following equations:

$$\text{For } Xi = X1 \ \frac{-5}{X_1{}^2} + 300\lambda = 0 \qquad \text{(A)}$$

$$= X2 \ \frac{-5}{X_2{}^2} + 300\lambda = 0 \qquad \text{(B)}$$

$$= X3 \frac{-1}{X_3{}^2} + 160\lambda = 0 \tag{C}$$

$$= X4 \frac{-2}{X_4{}^2} + 140\lambda = 0 \tag{D}$$

The memory constraint equation is:

$$300X_1 + 300X_2 + 160X_3 + 140X_4 = 10,000 \tag{E}$$

Using elementary algebra, the five equations with five unknowns can be readily solved with λ being not physically significant.

The optimum blocking factors are:

$$X1 = 12.1 = 12$$
$$X2 = 12.1 = 12$$
$$X3 = \ \ 7.3 = \ \ 7$$
$$X4 = 11.2 = 11$$

Therefore, File 1 will contain 12 records/block and 1,800 bytes of storage plus another 1,800 for alternate area.

File 2 will be identical to file 1.

File 3 will contain 7 records/block and 560 bytes of storage plus 580 bytes for alternate.

File 4 will contain 11 records/block and 770 bytes plus 770 for alternate.

The DOS FORTRAN program following will solve this problem for a program utilizing up to 6 tape files.

Input to it are two data cards as follows:

Card 1
    cc 1 Number of tape files.

Card 2
    cc 1–3 Memory available (in thousands of bytes)
    cc 4–7 Bytes per record File 1
    cc 8–11 Records per file File 1 (in thousands)
    cc 12–19 Same as 4–11 for File 2
    cc 20–27 Same as 4–11 for File 3
    cc 28–35 Same as 4–11 for File 4

cc 36–43 Same as 4-11 for File 5
cc 44–51 Same as 4-11 for File 6

```
0001        DIMENSION  BK(6),T(6),X(6), A(6), B(6)
0002        READ(1,101)N
0003  101 FORMAT(I1)
0004        READ(1,102)G,(A(I),B(I),I=1,N)
    C INPUT MEMORY F3.0,A(1) F6.0,B(1) F6.0,
    C        A(2) F6.0,B(2) F6.0, ETC
0005  102 FORMAT(F3.0,12F6.0)
    C CORE*1000 FOR INPUT SCALING DIVIDED
    C        BY TWO FOR ALTERNATE AREAS
0006        GK=500.*G
0007        DO 110 I=1,N
0008        BK(I)=B(1)*1000.
0009  110 CONTINUE
0010        DO 120 I=1,N
0011        T(I)=SORT(A(I)*BK(I))
0012  120 CONTINUE
0013        S=0.
0014        DO 130 I=1,N
0015        S=T(I)+S
0016  130 CONTINUE
0017        W=S/GK
0018        WRITE(3,190)W,GK
0019  190 FORMAT(F6.2,F6.2)
0020  140 DO 150 I=1,N
0021        X(I)=SQRT(BK(I))/(SQRT(A(I))*W)
0022        WRITE(3,180)I,X(I)
0023  180 FORMAT(3X,'FILE NBR',I1,'BLOCKING
              ',F6.1,'RECORDS PER BLOCK')
0024  150 CONTINUE
0025        STOP
0026        END
```

Index